DATE			

CALL OF DUTY

CALL
OF
DUTY

A Montana Girl
in World War II

GRACE PORTER MILLER

Foreword by

LINDA GRANT DE PAUW

LOUISIANA STATE UNIVERSITY PRESS
Baton Rouge

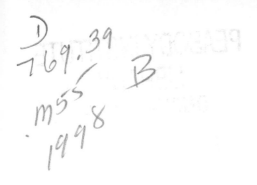

Copyright © 1999 by Louisiana State University Press
All rights reserved
Manufactured in the United States of America
First printing
99 01 03 05 07 08 06 04 02 00
1 3 5 4 2

Designer: Melanie O'Quinn Samaha
Typeface: Goudy
Printer and binder: Edwards Brothers, Inc.

Library of Congress Cataloging-in-Publication Data:

Miller, Grace Porter, 1921–
    Call of duty : a Montana girl in World War II / Grace Porter
Miller ; foreword by Linda Grant De Pauw.
      p.   cm.
    ISBN 0-8071-2343-9 (cloth : alk. paper)
    1. Miller, Grace Porter, 1921–   . 2. United States. Army.
Women's Army Corps—Biography.   3. World War, 1939–1945—
Participation, Female.   4. World War, 1939–1945—Personal
narratives, American.   5. Women soldiers—United States—Biography.
I. Title
D769.39.M55   1998
940.54'1273—dc21   98-44086
                                                                            CIP

The paper in this book meets the guidelines for permanence and durability of the Committee on Production Guidelines for Book Longevity of the Council on Library Resources. ∞

To my four children, who pushed me and cheered me on to write about my WAC days, especially my son, David Miller, Ph.D. in English, who has spent many hours editing and word-processing this book

CONTENTS

ILLUSTRATIONS

CONTENTS

FOREWORD

Linda Grant De Pauw

Women have always been involved in war, but when war songs
were sung or history books were written, women disappeared
from the record. They have not always gone quietly into oblivion. Yet even when they strove to preserve their own military
history, women's narratives were ignored. Few military histori-
ans mentioned women except to make a joke of them. Books
like Grace Porter Miller's *Call of Duty: A Montana Girl in World
War II* give us reason to hope that this will not happen to the
women who served in World War II.

After the Civil War and World War I, American women
who participated in those wars produced a flood of memoirs.
Most were never published or were published privately in limited editions; few found places on the shelves of reference libraries. That a respected academic publisher, Louisiana State
University Press, is publishing Miller's memoir signals that writing of this kind is a legitimate part of history. In recent years
a number of other memoirs by women veterans of World War
II have been similarly legitimatized by university presses and
mainstream publishers. Even now, however, most such memoirs bear the imprint of small presses or remain unpublished,
put aside with family papers and unknown or unavailable to
the scholars who might otherwise make use of them.

Miller's memoir is particularly valuable because the lag of

over fifty years between her experience and her writing about it allowed her to discuss subjects that have only recently become acceptable for public discourse. Fifty years ago, for instance, as Miller points out, "nice girls" had never heard the word *lesbian*. They were taught to ignore instances of what is now called "sexual harassment," and many felt that rape or attempted rape was somehow their fault, to be denied or kept as a shameful secret. The style of most World War II memoirs by women is relentlessly upbeat and cheerful. The "girls" who served recorded only the sunny hours during the crusade to prevent totalitarianism from engulfing the globe. The contrast with memoirs from Vietnam-era women veterans, who saw the suffering and horror of military service in what seemed a meaningless conflict, is striking.

Writing in the last years of the century, Miller has the maturity and perspective to present a balanced account. Her style is generally lighthearted, but she does not shrink from confronting the dark side of her military experience. Although she does not use the words *post-traumatic stress disorder*, she mentions a number of experiences that left her with recurring nightmares, and she describes physical problems that developed during her service. After the war she and other women veterans got no help from Veterans Administration hospitals because there were no facilities to treat women. Miller writes frankly about the once-taboo topic of lesbians in the WAC and discusses premarital pregnancies, attempted rape, and menstruation, and gives detailed descriptions of bathroom facilities. At the end of her book she expresses anger at being treated as a "second-class soldier" by men who had seen less of the hardship of war than she had.

The women who served in World War II were a despised elite. Despite their outstanding qualifications and record of service, women in uniform were viciously slandered as "officers' whores" or worse during the war, and after the war the American Legion and Veterans of Foreign Wars refused to admit them to membership. Although the WACs were proud of their professionalism and service, it was always understood that a WAC was not a *soldier*. The Women's Army Corps and the other women's services did not become a permanent part of the military establishment until 1948, and the WAC administrative structure segregated women from the rest of the regular army until the corps was abolished in 1978. Even today, when women's service has expanded dramatically so that women fly combat aircraft in war zones over Iraq and Bosnia and command combatant ships at sea, their exclusion from some military jobs solely on the basis of gender stigmatizes all servicewomen as second class.

World War II was a watershed for American military women because of the degree to which they were recognized as an official part of the army. From the beginning of American history, women served with the army, but few were considered part of it. The Articles of War, the governing law for the army, recognized civilians, both male and female, associated with military units as *camp followers*. They could not be called upon to perform military duty, but they were subject to military law and might be required to do nursing or similar noncombatant work. In addition, each regiment had a quota of "women of the army" or "laundresses" who were appointed to a limited number of positions and were paid by the military. These women, wives of the most deserving soldiers and selected because of their diligence and good character, lived on post and accompanied the marching army, doing nursing and other "women's work" as well as washing. They considered themselves members of the regiment, as did their male comrades. Almost half a century before the establishment of the Army Nurse Corps, women were buried in Arlington National Cemetery under headstones marked "Army Nurse." But the status of these army women was not equivalent to that of soldiers; it more closely resembled that of cavalry horses. They were at once indispensable and insignificant.

During the American Revolution and the Civil War, some camp followers wore male clothing, participated in drill, and even took part in combat without formally enlisting in the army. Other women assumed a male name along with male dress and took the enlistment oath. They became regular soldiers, but at the expense of losing their identity as women. After the Civil War, the military modernized and assigned to uniformed members tasks that had earlier been performed by laundresses. For a brief period the U.S. Army had no women serving. In 1874 the position of laundress was abolished, and when the United States went to war against Spain in 1898, the need for professional nurses to meet military needs was met by 1,200 civilian women volunteers recruited by the Daughters of the American Revolution. Not until 1901 was the Army Nurse Corps established, and then only as a quasi-official military organization that gave its members no military rank or benefits.

During World War I, faced with a need for women's services in a military that required experts in the use of modern technological devices such as typewriters and telephones, the navy was authorized to recruit women as Yeoman (F). The army had no such authorization but faced, perhaps, an even greater need. On the front lines in Europe, General John Joseph Pershing needed bilingual telephone operators to keep communications open. Operating telephones was women's work, so he proceeded without authorization and recruited women for service in the Signal Corps. Recruits were sworn into the service, wore uniforms, and served at switchboards within range of heavy artillery and gas attacks, with helmets and gas masks slung behind their chairs. After the war, they were retroactively civilianized, declared to have been "contract employees" although none had signed a contract. In 1977 Congress granted those still alive veteran equivalent status, but they have never been recognized as what they were: enlisted soldiers.

During World War II, the need for women's service was even more pressing, but the army resisted giving women military status. As Miller tells us, the army first recruited women as WAAC—the Women's Army Auxiliary Corps—classifying them as civilians. Members of the WAAC had no legal connection to the military and could leave the service any time they pleased. It took more than a year before the WAAC became the WAC—Women's Army Corps—with full military status and legal obligations.

Fifty years ago, women accepted demeaning inequality as natural or at least inevitable. Looking back, Miller now finds it galling. Thanks to her anger, we have this valuable book. May it not only give younger Americans new insight into the war that was the pivotal event of the twentieth century, but also inspire other women veterans to write or taperecord their recollections so that the fullest possible record of women's participation in these historic events will be preserved for posterity.

PREFACE

It was January 1943. The people of the United States had begun to realize that World War II was a life-or-death struggle to save world civilization. In Europe, the United States had just begun to fight the evil of the Nazi regime in Germany. In the Pacific, U.S. forces were engaged in combat against Japanese aggressors. A little over a year before, the Japanese sneak attack on Pearl Harbor had jolted the whole country into an awareness of how serious our nation's situation really was. Now the news on all fronts—North Africa, Southern Europe, Russia, and the Pacific—was extremely grave for the Allies.

I was young and bursting with patriotism. I had that youthful feeling that nothing bad could ever happen to me.

So I joined the army.

And I found out that I did *not* have that magic circle of protection surrounding me after all. Being in the United States Women's Army Corps during World War II was high adventure with lots of fun and travel. But sad things, painful things, horrifying things were also part of the package.

For me, life as a WAC meant:

. . . *feeling like a second-class member of the army.*

. . . *making wonderful new friends from all parts of the country and from all walks of life.*

. . . *suffering from blisters after long hikes in ill-fitting shoes.*

. . . *enjoying lots of parties and dancing and fun.*

. . . *working long, exhausting hours.*

. . . *ignoring scurrilous remarks about the morals of WACs from male soldiers as well as from some civilians.*

. . . *making the most of a chance to see a great deal of the United States and Europe.*

. . . *enduring bombing raids and getting lost behind enemy lines in the middle of the night.*

. . . *knowing that we were witnessing firsthand a dramatic part of history.*

. . . *seeing the sufferings of the people of Europe, especially the long lines of refugees.*

. . . *recoiling from the soul-wrenching sight of mass graves.*

. . . *joy riding in small planes with Air Force buddies.*

. . . *shuddering at the horror of the Dachau concentration camp.*

. . . *glowing in the good will that came with an armful of flowers from a stranger in France after V-E Day.*

. . . *bearing health problems caused by stress and poor food.*

Finally, when I came home again, much wiser, much more disillusioned than when I signed those papers in the recruitment office that made me a WAAC, I found that most Americans, including our government, usually did not consider servicewomen to be veterans.

I am proud to have been a member of the Women's Army Corps, but the price I paid to serve my country has been high.

So why did I enlist in the army? Why did I volunteer three times—first to join the WAAC (Women's Army Auxiliary Corps); second to join the WAC (Women's Army Corps); third to go overseas? When I ask myself these questions, I can only answer, *Because I am an American. And I love my country.*

ACKNOWLEDGMENTS

Thanks to Art, Bob, Jim, Glencora, and other members of the Prescott, Arizona, Mile-High Writers Club, who have helped me write and rewrite my stories. Thanks also to Donald Rule and his late wife, Verna Newman Rule, for use of photographs taken while we were all stationed in Belgium (my own pictures were all destroyed in a fire). My gratitude is also extended to the many Prescott people who have listened to me read these stories and have encouraged me to try to get them printed.

Last, I wish to thank Ms. Sylvia Frank, acquisitions editor for Louisiana State University Press, for her help in getting this printed and for her enthusiasm about my book.

Most of the names mentioned in this book are correct, but a few have been changed to avoid embarrassment to the persons or to their families, or simply because I have forgotten their names in the fifty years since I knew them. However, the events are written as they really happened.

CALL OF DUTY

1

"YOU'RE IN THE ARMY NOW!"

THE *QUEEN* AND THE SUBMARINE

By February 1944 I had been in the army for one year. Now I was one of forty Women's Army Corps members on board the former luxury liner Queen Mary. We were on our way to England with several thousand male GIs to supplement the American forces preparing for D-day.

All of the little group of WACs who were not suffering from seasickness were trying to eat our night meal. The *Queen Mary's* English crew had set up our mess hall in what had once been a swimming pool deep inside the huge ocean liner. Suddenly, a ship's officer appeared in the doorway.

"Attention! I must ask all of you to return to your cabins *at once.*" The urgency in his voice was accentuated by his clipped English accent. "You must be *absolutely quiet* until further notice. We have just discovered an enemy submarine in our close vicinity. All motors on the ship have been shut down and all communications have ceased. We ask you to please cooperate for the safety of everyone aboard. Return to your cabins *immediately*. No talking. No noise *whatsoever*. Put on your life jackets. Go to your bunks at once and remain there until further notification. We are going into total blackout in exactly one

1

minute. Please accomplish these orders with all possible speed. And you MUST *be absolutely quiet!"*

The sudden silence of the giant ship was eerie. No motors. No clatter of footsteps. No talk. Total silence punctuated only by the slapping of waves against the ship, the rolling and creaking of beams, and the pounding of our hearts. No lights, except for very dim lights in the lowest passageways where the light beams could not possibly reach the outside. It was as though the whole ship, with everyone on it, was dead and wallowing in the water. Everyone strained to hear the sound of a submarine engine. Our life jackets made any semblance of comfort impossible. No one slept. We hardly dared breathe. We lay there in our bunks, staring up at the dark ceiling, trying not to let our imaginations get the best of us, mentally reviewing the passageways and decks between us and the nearest lifeboat as we waited for an explosion.

The stillness lasted for long, agonizing hours, which seemed even longer in our anxiety. At last the ship eased slowly back to life, cautiously resuming its zigzagging course eastward. Officers came around to tell us we could talk now and could take off our life jackets. "But please keep all noise and lights at the barest minimum for a few more hours."

The Nazi sub had passed by in the night without spotting us!

For years, I did not realize what an extraordinary event this was, but I have since been told that this was the only time during World War II that either the *Queen Mary* or her sister ship, the *Queen Elizabeth*, was really threatened by German submarines. It was just happenstance that I was on the ship while she was in such grave danger.

As we tried to settle down to sleep after the officer left, I lay there in my bunk thinking about how amazing it was that this was happening to me. How had a shy girl from a Montana ranch become involved in a world war? And what further adventures and dangers lay ahead for me?

MY FIRST DAY AS A SOLDIER

President Franklin D. Roosevelt signed legislation creating the United States Women's Army Auxiliary Corps (WAAC) on May 15, 1942. From the beginning the organization was conceived as a second-class branch of the army, its "helping arm," not to be confused with "real" units of the U.S. Army.

On March 5, 1943, I was twenty-one years old, the minimum age at which women could enlist in the armed services, and I had just been stripped of civilianhood at Fort Des Moines, Iowa.

The six-foot two-inch, tough-talking sergeant's no-nonsense look relaxed for a moment. She smiled slightly as she looked at each new recruit lined up before her. "You are now members of the United States Women's Army Auxiliary Corps," she said in a voice momentarily soft. "Congratulations. And welcome!"

I was now officially "Private Grace Porter, dog tag number A-702462." A rush of pride, patriotism, and apprehension made me dizzy for a moment.

Then panic struck.

Had I made the right decision in volunteering for the army? As independent and stubborn as I was, would I be able to accept the orders and the total control of army life? What if I couldn't stand the army discipline . . . and then couldn't get out? Could I accept not being in charge of my future?

Now, fifty years later, I wonder if I would have joined the army that day had I known the misery, danger, and anguish I would encounter in the following months and years. After consideration, I always return to the same answer: *Yes. I would have volunteered, even knowing what lay ahead, because those years also held a large measure of fun and friendship, and the satisfaction of useful service during the years when my country needed all the help it could get.*

"Well," I thought, "it's too late now to back out. Might as well do my best and hope it works out all right." My mind wandered for a moment. A bright vision of me wearing a general's uniform appeared before my eyes. I was wearing shining medals from shoulder to waist, leading my own private ticker tape parade as I gallantly returned home at the end of the war. I stood straight and tall and proud as I shook the president's hand while he thanked me for my extremely important contribution to our country's victory over evil. *Ah, yes,* I murmured graciously: *No sacrifice is too much to preserve our freedom and our great country.*

My dream of future glory was abruptly ended by the sergeant's harsh bark: "All right, you recruits! Shape up! You're in the army now. All of you line up according to height. Tallest on the left. And don't waste any time doing it."

I was always the tallest girl in my high school and college classes, so I obediently went to the head of the line.

"I SAID, line up according to height. Tallest at the left."

I peeked down the line to see the eight-ball who was disobeying our first army order. It looked to me like everyone was in the right place. I turned my eyes to the front and tried to stand straight as a soldier should. Out of the corner of my eye I could see the sergeant's face turning an apoplectic red.

"Can't you damn recruits understand plain English? Line up by height. NOW! *And I mean YOU!*"

Her outstretched finger pointed directly at me! Shocked, I looked at the line again. Sure enough: the girl next to me was taller than I. And so were the next two! When I moved to fourth place, the sergeant was finally satisfied. She proceeded with the orders of the day, which I heard only vaguely through a happy haze.

All my life I had felt that I was the biggest and most awkward girl on earth. My growth had come early, so all through high school, at five foot nine inches, I was taller than all the other girls and most of the boys. I wasn't fat or misshapen—just *tall*—and very self-conscious about it. And now, here I was, *fourth* in line! Such a lovely feeling! And what a happy way to start my army career. I was no longer "that big one at the head of the line."

The warm glow wore off in a hurry as the problems and miseries of basic training began.

It didn't take long to settle in to the routines of army life with new friends, experiences, and vocabulary. We quickly learned that SNAFU meant "situation normal, all fouled up" (the mild version), Kilroy had been everywhere, and SOS was "shit on a shingle" (creamed dried beef on toast).

"Eager beaver," "goldbricking," "latrine rumors," "counting cadence," "GI runs," "SOP" (standard operating procedure), "TS" (tough shit), "policing the area," and many other army idioms soon became familiar.

The *Stars and Stripes* newspaper kept us posted on what was going on in the world.

We also learned the old army game of scrounging to secure the necessary items to make our barracks more attractive and comfortable. This skill was to serve us well throughout our army careers.

BASIC TRAINING

Every serviceman gripes about this miserable experience. Contrary to common assumptions, women recruits endured the same hardships and discipline as male recruits, with a few exceptions: no twenty-mile hikes—just ten-mile hikes. The obstacle courses we used were only a bit less strenuous than those used by men. No weapons or tactical training. But the same aching muscles and blistered feet. No softening of conditions or rules just because we were female: *You are soldiers in the United States Women's Army Auxiliary Corps, and you* WILL *learn to behave like U.S. soldiers.* It was made clear to us that we had given up the right to make our own decisions "for the duration." Our lives were irrevocably under the control of the army, and we had to do exactly as we were ordered or bear unpleasant consequences: extra KP (kitchen police) duty, or the honor of spending a few hours picking up all cigarette butts and matchsticks within a five-hundred-foot radius of our barracks.

Our hair always had to be "above the collar." No bangs or fancy styles. (At least we weren't scalped like the men.) Not too much makeup. Nails short, with no bright polish. No jewelry. Those first ill-fitting khaki uniforms must be spotless and without a wrinkle. (I could only dream of the brightly colored dresses I left at home.) Our ugly hats must have their bills at the exact proper angle. Our low-heeled, practical army shoes must be spit-polished to mirror brightness at all times. Seams on our khaki-colored cotton stockings must be ruler-straight— even if your legs were crooked! (How I missed my high heels and silk stockings.) And we had to practice for hours to get our arms and elbows at the proper angle to salute any officers we might encounter. Over and over we practiced, until we found ourselves saluting even sergeants and flagpoles.

We also had to practice reciting our dog tag numbers until they were completely automatic responses. Dog tags must be worn at all times—even in the shower! Those small metal disks were cold on your chest in winter weather, so one girl developed quite a business crocheting dog tag booties. Khaki colored, of course.

On arriving at Fort Des Moines, we each received new army wardrobes. "It's like going through a factory assembly line," someone murmured as we lined up in the supply room.

First, each WAAC was issued a barracks bag, and then she proceeded down the long counter manned by male army personnel. It was the first of many "line up and wait" experiences in the army.

After a few hours of shuffling, each of us had received uniforms, everything color-coordinated in fashionable khaki:

- six rayon panties (issuing personnel called them by their true army name, drawers);

- two suits of pajamas, cotton, peach-colored seersucker, "butcher boy" style;
- two suits of pajamas, blue and white checked flannelette, for winter;
- three slips, khaki rayon jersey;
- eight pairs of cotton hose, tan;
- eight pairs of rayon hose, tan;
- two girdles (khaki, of course);
- three brassieres, olive drab.

The bras were issued by a young, bashful army private. The poor boy was so embarrassed he could only hope to hurry through his job as quickly as possible. He gave a fast sidelong glance at each WAAC recruit, then shoved three of the items across the counter. A-cups were sometimes issued D-cups, and vice versa. So some of us needed to fill our cups with Kleenex, and some of us bulged obscenely over the top. (We later traded as best we could.) We felt sorry for (and amused by) that red-faced, sweating GI.

"Don't complain. You got three, didn't you? Just be sure you have the correct number of items allowed you," the sergeant ordered. "If there are any mistakes in sizes, they can be corrected later." "*If,*" she had said. Nothing we were issued seemed the right size! Especially those brassieres.

The shoe department had a measuring machine. Each WAAC was issued two pairs of leather shoes (with plenty of extra room for marching), one pair of athletic shoes, and galoshes. To my chagrin, I was issued size eights, instead of size six and a halfs. (What was worse, they almost fit when I wore several pairs of heavy socks to prevent blisters.)

In the millinery department we received khaki-colored dress caps fashioned after the French kepi, with a bill in front (nicknamed the Hobby hat after WAAC director Oveta Culp Hobby). A floppy fatigue hat resembling a limp tennis hat was also handed to each of us.

Uniforms included khaki summer blouses (shirts) and skirts. Winter uniforms of dark olive drab (OD) included two blouses and three skirts, a heavy warm overcoat, and a utility coat. The utility coat had a twelve-ounce wool interlining, which was removable so the coat could also serve as a raincoat. Warm woolen ski pants were also issued for winter wear.

The uniforms were made by men's tailors. Shoulders were wide, chests flat. Skirts were skinny. Breast pocket flaps on shirts had a tendency to stand straight out on any girl wearing anything larger than an A cup.

All this gear, whether it fit or not, got stuffed into the barracks bags, and off we were marched to our assigned barracks.

One hundred girls, sleeping in double-deck bunks, lived in each barracks. A wake-up bugle call began each day promptly at 5:45 A.M. Fifteen minutes later we lined up for roll call in front of our barracks, neat and fully dressed in the uniform of the day. March and April weather in Iowa is fickle, but no matter whether it was raining or snowing or blowing, we stood there at attention, shivering, stomachs growling, yearning for our warm cots. After roll call and the reading of the orders of the day, we spent fifteen minutes policing the area for cigarette butts and tiny bits of stray paper.

At 6:30, we were marched half a mile through ice, snow, or mud, usually on the double, to the mess hall for breakfast at 6:45. By that time, even the semiwarmth of the mess hall and the rough wooden benches and tables looked good. Lukewarm army coffee (awful!) was drunk in huge doses out of metal cups. Mountains of gray, greasy, ugly food served on metal trays were shoveled down—again in huge doses. This was no place for picky appetites. We needed a solid breakfast to keep us going until noon.

Those unlucky enough to be put on KP for the day were rousted out of bed an hour before everyone else and sent to the mess hall before the rest of us were awakened. KP was pure misery, and everyone had a turn at least once a week. Huge pots and pans, some big enough to crawl into, had to be scrubbed clean of accumulated gunk and burned-on food. (There went my manicure!) The grease traps on the immense stoves had to be emptied and cleaned, and their thick, yellowish-brown, rancid grease scooped into giant garbage barrels in the back of the kitchen. This job was done quickly, with breath held: The smell was nauseating and penetrated your whole body.

Tables had to be washed and hundreds of smelly ashtrays emptied. The sickening smell of those wet cigarettes and ashes guaranteed that I would always be a nonsmoker. Long wooden benches had to be upturned on top of the tables so the rough floors could be swept and mopped with big, heavy rag mops. Heavy, thick army dishes had to be washed and stacked—millions of them! All this had to be done under constant, nagging, abusive supervision by the cooks and their helpers. It seemed to us that it must have been obligatory for all army cooks to have vile tempers, savage tongues, and built-in hatred for everyone. Anyone who objected or grumbled pulled extra days of KP, so we worked in silence, trying desperately to keep out of their way. The banging of the pots and pans, the yelling of the cooks, the awful smells, and the clatter of the heavy dishes were sure to give us headaches.

By the end of twelve hours, the poor KP recruit was exhausted, barely able to crawl back to the barracks for the necessary very long, hot, soapy shower and blissful sleep that would follow, with dreams of someone else having KP tomorrow—or better yet, dreams of being able to supervise the *cooks* on KP. Hah! See if they'd like cleaning grease traps! We had a hard time smiling when some joker pretended to be the sergeant and yelled "Attention! Does anyone know shorthand? They're shorthanded in the mess hall!"

After breakfast the rest of us marched back to the barracks in time to prepare for inspection at 7:15. The only way to get out of inspection was to show up at sick call—but you'd better be sick! We may have been slobs at home, but the army demanded immediate perfection—we had to become instant spit-and-polish experts! Beds were arranged army style: "head to foot." The top blanket on each army cot had to be so tight that a dime dropped on it would bounce. Woe be unto anyone with a wrinkle on her bed or a corner that was not a precise hospital fold. And the blanket had to be double-folded at the top *exactly* six inches from the pillow.

The footlocker at the aisle end of the cot had to be open, with all possessions showing in perfect army order, no unauthorized knickknack or civilian object in view. All pictures had to be stuffed into barracks bags, out of sight. Shoes were lined up perfectly under the bed. Clothes were hung in open wall lockers in the exact prescribed order, every button buttoned. And, heaven forbid, NO DUST ANYWHERE.

Additional duties were doled out to everyone after breakfast. Some were assigned latrine duty to ensure that our bathrooms were spotless and shining. The world's most persnickety surgeon could perform appendectomies on our bathroom (better known as latrine) floor by inspection time. We learned the hard way how to clean shower, sink, and toilet bowl so that even the cracks shone in pristine whiteness. Mirrors glistened bright enough to hurt your eyes—absolutely NO streaks. An old toothbrush worked wonders in cracks around faucets. A Kotex and some elbow grease ensured spotless, streakless mirrors and windows. Other recruits policed the grounds some more. No matchsticks!

When the inspecting officers arrived at our barracks, all one hundred of us jumped to attention at the foot of our beds. Long rows of women stood there, eyes straight ahead, shoulders back, feet with heels together, toes at the exact angle apart, everything color coordinated: khaki blankets, khaki footlockers, lovely khaki uniforms (even our stockings, underwear, and girdles). Everything was pressed correctly: The only thing allowed to be wrinkled was our brow. We spent hours every evening washing and pressing carefully. Men in the army received laundry service, but we washed our own clothes.

The inspectors scrutinized each window sill, footlocker, bed, shoe, and WAAC for any possible slipup. There were usually four officers in the inspection team, two WAAC officers and two male army officers. They wore white gloves to check for traces of dust on bed springs, door frames, and other unlikely places. It was amazing how ingenious these inspecting officers could be in finding dust or trivial imperfections. I often wondered if their own quarters were as nearly perfect as our barracks. Who inspected their quarters? If they were married, I sympathized with their poor wives or husbands.

When the inspectors moved on to the next barracks, a great sigh came from everyone. Hurray! We had passed inspection. No extra KP for today! Even if the barracks as a whole passed, there was usually some poor girl caught with her hair a sixteenth of an inch too long, or her shoes not quite shiny enough or slightly out of line, or with a speck of dust somewhere in her vicinity. In our company, it always seemed to be Susie Ranton, a good-natured, slapdash recruit from Tennessee who, in spite of all her efforts to be perfect, somehow managed to leave a shoe untied, or the edge of a picture of her family showing, or some dust on the upper windowsill by her bed, or her khaki tie tucked between the third and fourth buttons of her shirt instead of the proper second and third buttons, or the knot in her tie too loose.

She would be assigned to extra KP. I would feel sorry for her (with secret relief that it wasn't me). Each day dread kept me from breathing normally during this intensive scrutiny, but I was never unlucky enough to be caught for anything important.

Following inspection, we were given a few minutes at ease, then lined up outside to march to classes. The rest of the day was spent in various military classes (army history classes, classes on customs and courtesies of the army, long lectures on the Articles of War, army office procedures) and exercises (drilling practice, calisthenics, running obstacle courses, or long marches). Some of the classes were boring, but we were full of enthusiasm and anxious to do a good job in our new life, so we tried hard to assimilate all this information.

When classes ended at 1630 hours, we marched back to our barracks. We were given fifteen minutes to go to the bathroom, read the latest regulations and the KP list on the bulletin board, and wash up for supper. We stood for retreat as the sun set over the post, then marched to supper to the music of a brassy-voiced squad leader counting cadence. Tired as we were, we still wolfed down the army chow. We griped—but we ate the stuff. Seconds, too, if we could get them. Army life requires plenty of courage, stamina, and a boiler-plate stomach. The stomach on which the U.S. Army marches is filled with greasy potatoes and stale, bitter coffee.

Classes were even held after supper. We were shown *Loose Lips Sink Ships*, or movies about VD, and news clips about Hitler and the bombings in Europe and Pearl Harbor. Before lights-out at 10:00 P.M., there was usually a little free time. A few minutes for washing and ironing. Time for a shower in the curtain-free shower room. The army is no place for shrinking violets: We lived like goldfish, even in the shower. We didn't even have shades on our windows.

We were usually too tired for much social life, but those evenings gave us a chance to get acquainted with our barracks mates. My new friends came from all parts of the country, all levels of education and experience, all walks of life, and from various races and cultures. It was an unlikely collection of people, but we learned to get along with each other. Evenings were the time to gripe about the trials of the day; griping relieved the tensions and frustrations we all felt in this new life.

Somehow it is much easier to endure hardships if you can complain to someone stuck in the same boat who can understand just how you feel and can sympathize a bit. The women recruits rapidly became adept at the old army game of griping about the army and its officers.

Taps sounded at 10:00 P.M., and we were eager for those narrow, hard army cots and scratchy army blankets. Taps—so sad and sweet as you lay there, bone-tired, lonesome, dreaming of home and loved ones, but with a feeling of togetherness with your barracks mates.

There was surprisingly little friction between the girls, especially considering the diversity of backgrounds. The WAAC was a new outfit, and we all were excited at being part of it, anxious to do our best to live up to its standards, and a little afraid of this complete change in our lives. The result was that we were pulled together, not apart, and soon became a unit.

At first, there were no blacks in our company at Fort Des Moines, but while we were there a group of black recruits (mainly from Chicago) came in. Our only contact with them was in the mess hall. On our family ranch in Montana near a mining town filled with people from all over the world, I had been taught to judge people by their actions rather than by the color of their skins. I was willing to accept these recruits as equals. However, since I had always lived in small towns, I was not prepared for big-city aggressiveness. The Chicago recruits were used to pushing and shoving to get a good place in line—which offended me. However, there were no serious confrontations. We learned later that these black recruits had been sent to a motor pool company in Texas. I don't remember seeing any black women soldiers the rest of the time I was in the army.

Fort Des Moines, the first training center set up for the WAACs, began classes on July 20, 1942. The second training center was at Daytona Beach, Florida, and the third training center was at Fort Oglethorpe, Georgia.

Officers had been trained first, then recruits. My basic training company was one of the first groups of enlisted women to be trained at Fort Des Moines. This was a large but beautiful old army cavalry post, set up efficiently with rows and rows of brick barracks that looked like horse barns, and acres of drill fields spread in all directions. Huge officers' quarters stood in long rows on tree-lined streets.

Long hours of drilling every day soon whipped us into sharp marching teams:

"Hut, two, three, four. Hut. Hut. Hut, 'hoo, 'hree, 'hore. Hut. Hut . . ."

We heard the sergeant barking orders even in our sleep (no one in the army seemed to speak: They just barked or shouted): "To the rear. March. To the left flank. Harch. To the right flank. Harch. To the rear. Harch."

On and on we marched each day until our eyes glazed and our blisters bled. Better pay close attention! A missed "To the rear. March" and you were suddenly face to face with a long file of fellow marchers, all intent on following orders and tramping straight ahead . . . right over or through you if necessary. Or worse yet, the poor soul who found herself marching smartly to the left flank . . . all alone in the middle of the drill field while the rest of the company marched off into the sunset on a "To the right flank. March." Ah, the loneliness of it! Followed closely, of course, by the sergeant's "Company! Halt!" Then a bellow of rage aimed in the miscreant's direction. There was no way to sneak quietly back into line, no shelter from the sergeant's blistering comments on the total and complete stupidity of some jackass recruits who didn't know their left foot from their right foot or their ass from a hole in the ground.

Sergeants saw everything, everywhere. Would we ever have peace or privacy again? Someone (I can't remember who) once wrote that in basic training "persecution is deliberate, calculated, systematic." Routine was as inhuman as an industrial production line. The army had a reason for everything, whether it made sense or not. And the sergeants were there to see that we damn well adhered to each and every army rule and regulation in the book—or else. It seemed as though the sergeants' basic purpose was to make our lives miserable. However, under their tutelage we quickly learned a lot about army life and discipline.

Fourteen weeks later, it was worth all this misery. WAAC units were asked to march in a parade, and we did, looking neat, precise, and proud! As an army band played a Sousa march, the thrill and pride of being a member of the U.S. armed forces spread wide and deep through each one of us. We knew we loved our homeland enough to give our lives for it if necessary. We *knew* why we had joined the army, and it was a good feeling. We had become soldiers.

"WHY"

I was a young schoolteacher in Manly, Iowa, before I joined the army. Many of the young men had gone into the armed services, so my social life was quiet, proper, dull. As a popular song said, "They're either too young or too old, They're either too bald or too bold." Weekdays my second graders kept me busy. Weekends were spent issuing ration cards at the school or helping to scour the countryside for unused metal. Bridge games with other teachers, movies, and long walks occupied my time.

Then one day the rumor circulated that all teachers' positions would soon be frozen for the duration. The thought of being caught in this net alarmed me greatly. I liked my job, but after a year and a half in Manly, and after teaching since I was seventeen, I knew I didn't want to spend the rest of my life with second graders. For several years I had watched all the boys I knew marching off to the army or navy, and I had envied them their chance to DO something about this terrible struggle in which our world was involved. If I became trapped in this static position, I could never do much to help the war effort. In October 1942, I celebrated my twenty-first birthday and thereby became eligible to join one of the women's services. Joining up seemed the logical thing to do. Keeping the home fires burning was fine for some, but I could not bear the thought of being so passive and so out of touch with the action. Paper drives were not enough for me.

The next day after the position-freezing rumor came out, I sent in an application to the Women's Marine Corps. Those marine uniforms were so classy! And I looked so good in blue! Orders soon came to report for a physical. I passed with flying colors . . . except for my eyes. I was just a bit too nearsighted to meet marine standards. The medical officer who examined me suggested that I go home, eat carrots and drink carrot juice for a week, then try again. Carotene might make the difference. For one week I gagged down carrot juice by the gallon. My skin literally turned yellow. When my vision was retested, sure enough, my eyes had improved. But still not quite enough to pass the test for the marines.

I was terribly disappointed, but determined. While I was still crammed full of carrots, I went over to the army recruiting office and passed their test. Their requirements for eyes were not quite so stringent as the marines', although the rest of the physical was the same. Army doctors performed physicals with a bemused look, after having dealt so long only with male recruits. Medical orderlies wandered through the army hospital halls with glazed looks as the women volunteers floated around in skimpy hospital gowns dubbed "angel robes."

Papers were signed. I was ordered to report to Fort Des Moines, Iowa, on the March 1. I had done it!

Although the school board in Manly was not too happy about losing a teacher, they were very nice about releasing me from my contract.

The weekend after I enlisted, I went home to break the news to my family.

I was the oldest of four children (three girls and a boy). In 1942, as soon as my brother turned eighteen, he had gone to enlist in the army but had been turned down because of a hernia. He cried when he got the rejection notice, and we cried with him.

The men in our family had always served in their country's wars. My father, a tall, handsome, powerfully built man with narrowed eyes, the Porter family's determined set of jaw, and a deep bass growl of a voice, had served under General Pershing in the Mexican border war in the pre–World War I years. As soon as the First World War began, he reenlisted in the army as a member of the Montana Regiment that saw action in most of the famous battles in Europe. During the battle of the Argonne Forest, he was gassed and spent several subsequent months at the army hospital in Vichy, France. He never talked about his war experiences, but once when I was young a group of men from the Montana Regiment came to our ranch near Roundup, Montana, to see my father and honor him. They called him a war hero. He had gone over the top of the trenches into no-man's-land under heavy German fire to pull back a severely wounded American soldier.

My dad, like me, had been raised on a ranch in Montana. He was the typical American soldier of his era: a dead shot who fought to win and knew how to do it; opinionated, independent, and ornery; completely honest, loyal, and generous; patriotic.

My parents were married shortly after Dad came home from France, and their romance lasted the rest of their lives, through the bad times of the depression when we lost our ranch, the times they both had to scramble to support us kids, and through serious illnesses. Dad worked hard in spite of being gassed in France, severe arthritis, and various aches and pains after being mashed against a corral fence by a big bull. My mother was a sweet, pretty, gentle, humorous woman with quiet, subtle ways. And an iron will! (My dad was recognized as the boss, but she ruled the roost.) My brother and sisters and I learned from them about duties in life and about morality. They also taught us that sometimes it is necessary to do without a lot of things and to work hard in order to achieve our goals in life.

In our family the women were always equal partners: Decisions were always made by the men and the women equally. When the women's liberation movement came along, it was a surprise to me. I had always felt equal to men (and maybe superior to some of them). I had been taught that I could be or could do anything I wanted to as long as I was willing to work and try my best. And I was encouraged to think for myself, not just to follow the crowd.

Women in my family were strong-willed and independent. Both sides of the family had come to this country from Europe in the ten or twenty years after the Mayflower. They raised large families in the New World's wilderness. After her husband's early death, one of my great-great-grandmothers took over as canalboat captain and raised a large family on their boat on the Erie Canal. Another was scalped by the Indians and left for dead, then led a long, busy life, wearing a cap to cover her scars. Several of my great grandmothers rode across the country in covered wagons. As a girl in West Virginia during the Civil War, my maternal grandmother lived in an area where the two armies took turns sweeping through and commandeering everything in sight. My gentle schoolmarm mother had carried a gun to protect herself from outlaws and wolves as she rode horseback across the Montana prairies to her schoolhouse.

So I had a long tradition of strong women to live up to. Also I was raised on our Montana ranch where I learned to be independent and self-reliant. Roundup, Montana, a rough mining town, offered few opportunities for "sissy stuff" for girls. If we showed signs of being squeamish or weak, we were teased unmercifully by our family and the cowboys. And my father favored strict "army" discipline for his family.

I was also used to changes and new challenges in my life. At age fifteen, I moved to Iowa to live on our grandfather's farm while I went to college. Before I was eighteen, I was teaching school in a small Iowa town.

With this background, I wasn't afraid to join the army or to face whatever army life might bring to me.

As I walked in our front door that Saturday in early 1943, I took a deep breath, crossed my fingers behind my back, and blurted "Mom. Dad. I have something important to tell you. I've enlisted in the WAACs."

Dad blinked several times, then beamed. "I'm proud of you, kid. Good luck!"

Mom didn't say anything for a long time. Just looked at me. Then, with a faint smile, she said, "Well, if I were your age, I'd do the same thing."

I was never more proud of my parents.

Now, over fifty years later, I know that many women find my reasons for joining the army incomprehensible, as did most women in 1942.

Most well-brought-up young women in the first half of this century were expected to get only enough education to help them become good wives and good mothers. A few brave souls wanted more in their lives, but the majority of women accepted such a social concept with only minor grumblings. Seeds of discontent leading to the women's lib movement were there, but few women were able yet to do much to change things.

When World War II intruded into our lives, I saw the women I knew being forced to take more active roles in society. Many of my friends, and even my younger sister, left home to work in defense industries or to take the place of men in other jobs. Families spread across the world to new jobs and new homes. The prewar closeness of most families was destroyed. Women were too far away from mothers or sisters or aunts to depend on easily available support, advice, and help. Women had to learn to cope with life as independent persons.

After World War II, many women became better educated

and began to choose their own ways of life, even when this led outside the home. Our lives became more complicated. Now we had to choose between being family-oriented or me-oriented, and the decisions were—and remain—difficult.

My mother's friends were baffled by girls enlisting in the army, although secretly they savored the adventure of it and admired our courage and independence. However, it was too much of a break with tradition for them even to contemplate it for themselves. Such independence was a frightening concept!

My daughters' generations are too far from the World War II era to grasp the fact that the war scared the hell out of us and made huge changes in the everyday lives of everyone in the country. Wars since then have been farther away, more detached. My daughters have never known the inconvenience of rationing everyday necessities like gasoline and butter and sugar and nylons, or the terrors of imminent bombings, invasion, or massive military defeat.

Women of my own generation generally accepted the idea of female soldiers as necessary. They understood why I joined the army, though most of them feared the hardships of army life and the criticism and slander to which women volunteers were subjected.

Joining the army seemed to me a very logical thing to do. We were in the midst of a war that involved the whole world. Everyone in the country felt the immediacy and desperation of our situation. We all saw it as a life-or-death struggle between the decent people of the world and the dark forces of evil and cruelty. It was easy to imagine what would happen to the world if Hitler, Hirohito, and their gangs won this war, which seemed very possible right then. The whole world, even our mighty United States, was in mortal danger. Every city and village in the country felt very threatened, especially since Pearl Harbor. Children woke at night with nightmares of being attacked by German storm troopers.

Every day, newspapers printed stories of atrocities being per-petrated on the helpless people of Europe. Millions of Jews were being tortured and killed. One European country after another was being invaded by Nazi storm troopers. London was bombed nightly and its citizens forced to spend long hours in bomb shel-ters. We saw pictures of English children being sent away from their families to safer countries. The U.S. government sent a boatload of Jewish refugees back to Europe, and our hearts ached for them as we realized it probably meant death for them. Allied troops were suffering defeats in battles in North Africa, the Mediterranean, and Italy. Tales were whispered of resis-tance fighters risking their lives every day in France and other Western European countries. News pictures of war and bombed cities horrified us. Adolf Hitler and his thugs strutting around giving their hysterical speeches and insane salutes sent cold shivers up and down our backs. Mesmerized German crowds responding like robots to Hitler's maniacal screams shocked, frightened, and bewildered us.

At home in the United States we felt fairly safe, but rumors had German U-boats prowling freely up and down our Atlantic coast in 1942. We found out later that from January to the end of May that year, eighty-seven ships were sunk in American waters, many within sight of land. Eastern beaches were lit-tered with tar and debris—and sometimes bodies—from mer-chant ships sunk by the German subs. Fear of Japanese subs ter-rified our western coast. On January 23, 1942, a Japanese submarine bombarded Santa Barbara, California, inflicting minor damage. Everyone was alerted to possible spy activities anywhere in the country. The growing chance of enemy attacks or bombings in the continental United States haunted our dreams. Volunteer "air spotter" groups were formed to watch the skies on both East and West coasts as well as inland—even my mother in Iowa studied warplane outlines in order to be able to identify enemy aircraft. Places with German or Japan-ese names were renamed, and there was prejudice against anyone who was German or Japanese. On Puget Sound, Washington, farmers with pitchforks and clubs patrolled up and down the beaches. We had begun to feel very vulnerable.

Throughout the country, politicians, ministers, and other speakers portrayed the war as a struggle between forces of freedom and decency and forces of slavery and terror. People believed this everywhere in the United States. We shared a new sense of unity and purpose.

In the previous decade, Franklin Delano Roosevelt had led us out of the depression and into an age of public cooperation. Under his leadership and New Deal policies, public works such as the Tennessee Valley Authority and the national roads systems were built, work programs such as the Works Progress Administration were created to give jobs to the unemployed. The Germans and Japanese did not understand how much the ordinary citizens of the United States loved and believed in FDR. When FDR—with the wholehearted support of the people—turned his organizational abilities to war efforts, the United States became an indomitable giant that was capable of crushing enemies on both sides. Besides, like FDR, we were furious at German treacheries in Europe and at Japan's sneak attack on Pearl Harbor. FDR was to us more than a man: He was us. We organized. We built. Men, women, children—all volunteered.

My mother's Methodist Church Circle rolled bandages and prepared Red Cross packages. Gasoline was closely rationed, as were many foods such as fats, sugar, and flour. The little Polish lady who lived near my parents had to stop making her beloved poteetsa. My first- and second-grade students rolled the foil from sticks of gum and cigarette packs into balls to be saved, and competed with each other to see who had the biggest ball. Every piece of unused junk metal was given to collection depots for manufacture of munitions or building of ships. Plowshares were, literally, beaten into guns. War bond drives brought in thousands of dollars each week to help support the tremendous costs of fielding an army. Everyone shared the deprivations and needs of our total war effort.

Worst, of course, were the long lists of U.S. casualties in daily newspapers. Blue stars appeared in many windows to denote homes where sons or husbands were away at war. Gold stars meant they were dead. Towns hastily erected honor rolls of servicemen who had been killed. Few families did not have someone in the army, navy, marines, coast guard, or merchant marine. Every family lived with the constant dread of receiving a telegram saying that their loved one was wounded or missing in action or killed. The most dreaded people in America were those delivering Western Union telegrams. Many older men were hired for this job, and they were encouraged to help grieving families as much as possible.

We were all in the war. The closeness and very possible danger to each of us and to our homes and country was an ever-present worry. We were afraid. Afraid enough to accept rationing and curfews. Afraid enough to try to do our individual best to support our armed forces and our government. This was a war that touched every U.S. citizen more closely and more completely than any war since.

This was the atmosphere of the country in the winter of 1942–1943.

So why did I enlist? Did I get paid well? *An auxiliary (private) in the WAACs received $50 a month. A sergeant got $78 per month, and a first lieutenant received $150 per month. Plus a free khaki wardrobe and all the army mess you could eat. Quite a pay cut, for most of us.*

Was it for fun and adventure? No. *(Well, maybe just a little bit.)*

Was it for the honor? *Definitely not! Women in uniform were regarded as second-class citizen-soldiers. As one writer (again, I apologize for not remembering who) put it, "They had to endure the wisecracks of their fellow GIs and the derision of civilians who alternately accused them of lesbianism and heterosexual promiscuity." We had to develop very thick skins to survive.*

Well, why *did* I enlist, then?

It was for love. For love of our country and our way of life, and for the safety of loved ones, all of which were being seriously threatened at that time. After all, women can be as patriotic as men.

"THE EYES OF TEXAS ARE UPON YOU"

Basic training had seemed to last forever and ever, but eventually it came to an end. On May 1, an anxious crowd gathered around our company bulletin board to check out the shipping lists just posted. Where would we go from here? Would we like it? Would we get to go with our friends? We could hardly wait to find out our assignments. Delighted screams and disgusted groans filled the air as the lists were read.

When I finally elbowed my way to within reading distance of the board, I was delighted to find that I was being sent to an army administration school at a women's college in Denton, Texas. So much for all my worry about cooks and bakers school. No eternal KP for me!

"Wow," exploded Dorothy, my favorite friend in basic. "We're *both* going to Denton!"

We did a little dance of joy, then started stuffing all our gear into our khaki duffel bags. I soon learned some real techniques for packing a duffel bag. All our army gear, clothing, mess kits, plus all our personal belongings, had to go into that one bag. And then the darn thing had to be carried by the owner, sometimes for miles. My fingers felt inches shorter from stuffing so much into so little space. They ached for months after each move from shoving and poking things down into those damn bags. We learned to pack very efficiently: Each shoe was stuffed full of socks or panties. There were no empty spaces left in any container or corner.

Before going to Denton, we were issued summer uniforms, so we had both summer and winter gear to more than fill all available space.

Two days later, six of us, loaded down with duffel bags,

boarded the train to Denton. From various basic training camps around the country, other groups joined us.

The Denton training center, with less than a hundred trainees, was set up on the campus of the Denton State Teachers College in North Texas. It was a lovely campus with old brick buildings and lots of trees and flowers.

As we walked up the front steps of the college (lugging those duffel bags), we were serenaded by a group of earlier trainees singing "The Eyes of Texas Are upon You." Corny, but sort of nice, and we felt welcome and special. After ego-busting basic, that felt great! We were assigned rooms in the college dormitory, two or three to a room. Sheer luxury! Even some privacy, at last! We ate in the college cafeteria, so no KP! Now we *knew* we were out of basic.

Six weeks of classes in army office procedures and army customs and practice were held for eight hours each day. The work was demanding, and quite a few were washed out along the way and sent on to other types of work.

Every morning for two hours before class, even though it was a hot, humid spring in Texas, we had to practice close order drill, dressed in full summer uniform, including long-sleeved shirts, ties (which I had finally learned to knot correctly), and long cotton stockings. Most of us were fresh from a cold northern winter. By the end of the two hours we could wring water out of those damn heavy stockings. Our entire uniforms were soaked with sweat, except for the bottom eight inches of skirt that flapped in the breeze. Before we could go to class, we had to shower and change right down to the skin.

Despite the discomfort, we enjoyed the marching because the sergeants encouraged us to do a lot of singing. Singing kept us in step and kept our minds off how hot we were. We developed quite a repertoire of army songs. Fun ones like:

Be kind to your web-footed friends,
For a duck may be somebody's mother.

> Be kind to your friends in the swamp,
> Where it's damp.
> You may think that this is the end.
> Well, it is.

We had fun with a few less proper songs, like:

> I wish I were a fascinatin' bitch.
> I'd never be poor, I'd always be rich.
> I'd live in a house with a little red light.
> I'd sleep all day, and I'd work all night.
> Take a vacation 'bout once a month,
> Just to drive my customers wild.
> I wish I were a fascinatin' bitch
> Instead of a legitimate child.

Or:

> If you're tired of Spam and powdered eggs,
> Have a baby! Have a baby!

Or the old army favorites, like:

> Gee, Ma, I wanta go home—

We had a busy schedule at Denton, but we had more time for recreation than in basic, so we could attend some of the army company parties we were invited to in the area. One day we even enjoyed boating on Lake Dallas with some soldiers from a nearby base.

In Denton, I began to encounter prejudice against, misinformation about, and stereotyping of women in the armed services. Thank goodness there were only a few ignorant, vicious individuals who smeared us, but they could, and occasionally did, make our lives miserable. Almost all the women I knew in the army were good, decent young women with high morals. Of course there were a few who did not measure up to this standard, but I know of no group anywhere, in politics, clubs, or churches, that does not include some sinners. In fairness, you should not judge an entire group by one or two misfits.

When some ignorant loudmouth would start to call us names, like "camp followers," "whores," or "dykes," some friendly soldiers or sailors or marines would always stand up for us.

"These are nice girls," they would shout. "They're helping us to fight this war, and you'd better shut your mouth or I'll shut it for you." The ignorant one would always back off as more servicemen came to our defense.

We hated these encounters, but it made us feel good to have so many decent men stand up for us. We also learned (the hard way) to ignore unjust criticism. We built shells around our inner selves to protect us from abuse. In a way, I have been grateful for this phase of army life because since then I have been able to face the unjust cruelties of life with more courage and aplomb. I learned that what people say is not always right or truthful, and I learned not to believe gossipers. There are always vicious people, but I do not have to listen to them or believe their lies and innuendoes. I learned the futility of fighting back with the same tactics, or with denials, which only fuel further problems. Doing what I thought was right and ignoring the lies seemed the best way to cope with these situations.

My clearest memories about my short stay in Denton are of my two roommates.

Dorothy had become my best friend while we were in basic at Fort Des Moines. We were delighted to be sent to the same school and doubly glad to be allowed to room together while we were there. She was a lovely blonde girl from Salt Lake, very sweet and naive, with a great sense of humor, and we enjoyed each other's companionship.

The dormitory was crowded, and we were assigned a large room, so after a day or two we were asked to make room for another roommate, a thin, dark, mannish woman in her late twenties, from New Jersey, who swaggered in and brusquely started taking over. Instinctively, neither of us liked her, but we tried to make her welcome and to get along with her.

As days went by, Claudia tried to make herself agreeable to both of us, but she was especially friendly to Dorothy. It soon dawned upon me that she was spending a lot of time trying to ingratiate herself with my roommate. At first she would do little things especially for Dorothy, like sharing cookies from home with her or cleaning Dorothy's side of the room. She was polite to me, but very cool and distant. Dorothy was embarrassed because I was being left out, but too polite to say anything.

Claudia gradually began lying around on Dorothy's bed, spending more and more time with her, talking or listening to the radio, giving Dorothy more and more friendly hugs and pats. For a while, neither Dorothy nor I realized what was going on. We were both young and very naive, and wanted to think the best of everyone. We really had no idea what was happening in our room. All our lives, we both had been taught good manners and courtesy. I had never come in contact with a lesbian on our ranch in Montana or as a teacher in Iowa—I hardly knew what the word meant. In the 1940s, most people were not as aware of homosexuality as we are in the 1990s. Such things were certainly not discussed in those days, especially in front of nice young women, so we were both "babes in the woods" about this subject.

Claudia got bolder and cuddlier every day. I think I caught on first, but I didn't know what to do. After all, Dorothy *seemed* to be enjoying the attention. Then the situation got more and more out of hand. Suddenly, Dorothy *knew*. We tried to talk about it without naming it, but didn't know enough about the subject to know what to say. We were too shocked and embarrassed to talk to anyone, even each other, about it. Dorothy began to have a desperate look and started staying out of the room as much as possible. Our roommate became angry and pushy. Dorothy was not getting enough sleep because every now and then during the night Claudia would rouse up and head for Dorothy's bed. As soon as she came near, Dorothy would say "Go away! I'm trying to sleep" in a loud voice so I'd be sure to wake up. "What's going on?" I would mumble sleepily. "Oh, I'm just going over to get a drink of water," Claudia would grumble. Dorothy would flick on the light until Claudia went back to her own bed, and then Dorothy and I would look at each other with relief and try to go back to sleep.

It is hard to say what the next step would have been. Both Dorothy and I were too embarrassed to go to our commanding officer about the problem as we should have done. Then, in June 1943, just as the school was almost completed, the army finally decided to accept the Women's Army Auxiliary Corps into its ranks as full-fledged soldiers. So, after six months in the army, we could now become members of the WAC (Women's Army Corps), a branch of the regular army with rank and pay status equal to other soldiers. Anyone who wanted to stay in had to reenlist. The others were mustered out and sent home as soon as the school ended. I signed up for the duration, but because of Claudia, Dorothy chose to go home. She had been enthusiastic about the army and her future in it, but this was a fast, easy way out of an uncomfortable and embarrassing situation. She was so ashamed and unhappy (although she was completely innocent) that even though we were very close friends, I never heard from her again. Fortunately, after I left Denton, I never saw Claudia again either.

Over the years since then, I have known other women who prefer women and have accepted some of them as friends, but never again have I met one so pushy and rude as Claudia. She was a sexual predator, apparently attracted to the WACs as an easy hunting ground. WACs often had to repulse male sexual predators, but we expected them and were prepared to deal with them. We were unprepared to deal with predators who were female.

The procedures required to transfer everyone from one branch to another had not been completed in Washington,

D.C., so I was still legally in the WAAC when I was sent to my first station at March Army Air Force Base outside Riverside, California. I was only at March for a couple of weeks en route to an assignment to San Diego, but they were interesting weeks.

Never will I forget the awe I felt as I saw the majestic rows of stately old palm trees swaying gently in the dry desert air at Riverside. I had spent all my life in the northern United States, so palm trees seemed exceedingly exotic and impressive.

It was also exciting to work in the squadron offices on the line at the airfield. There was paperwork to be done as well as a lot of errands to be run right in the immense hangers and on the field, so for the first time I was involved in regular air force work. It was thrilling beyond words. The roar of the B-17s, the busy maintenance crews, dashing around in jeeps—this was what I had dreamed about as an Iowa teacher. At last I felt I was a contributing part of the army! I was actually doing something useful for the war effort, no matter how unimportant my job was. At that stage in my career, even riding in a jeep to and from the hangers was exciting. The satisfaction I felt was enormous. My school teaching days seemed millenniums away.

LIFE IN THE ZOO

I was officially sworn into the regular U.S. Army as a member of the Women's Army Corps in San Diego on September 1, 1943. The WAAC had now officially become the WAC.

San Diego! Now *there* was a dream post for a WAC during wartime. I was based in that lovely city for almost a year . . . and what a fabulous year it was!

When I got orders for this choice assignment, I was the envy of everyone at March. My assignment in San Diego was in the inspector general's office. San Diego was the headquarters for a large number of air bases in southern California, all with planes and equipment requiring regular inspections and much paperwork. Most of my time was spent in the office working on reports, but now and then an inspecting officer needed someone to take notes, so I had the opportunity to visit many of the southern California air bases. It was exciting work, and I loved it.

The first six months I was there, our small company of thirty-five or forty WACs was billeted in barracks in the middle of Balboa Park in central San Diego, just across a small ravine from the lions' cages in the Balboa Park Zoo. Every morning we were awakened by the roaring of the lions as they awaited their breakfasts and by the parrots and other tropical birds screaming in their cages on another side of us.

It was a beautiful six-block walk down the hill and through the park to the headquarters where we worked.

Later, our WAC company was enlarged and extra room was needed, so during the last few months I was in San Diego some of us were housed several miles out toward the ocean on Point Loma. Our dormitory, on the campus of a girls' college, was named Quetzal Hall after the tropical quetzal bird. A huge painting of this exotic bird was in the main stairwell. The campus was lush, and the unbelievably strong, sweet smells of jasmine and other tropical flowers and bushes filled our nights.

San Diego has one of the best climates in the world, especially in fall, winter, and early spring. Soft air scented with tropical flowers, gentle sea breezes off the warm ocean current always keeping temperatures comfortable, low humidity, and lovely scenery with mountains on one side and the ocean on the other make it an ideal spot.

Office hours were nine to five, so we had a lot of free time for exploring the area and for dates and parties. Because it was the main jumping-off place for the Pacific theater of war, San Diego was swarming with sailors, marines, and even a few soldiers. Aside from nurses at the San Diego Naval Hospital, the WACs in our company were the only servicewomen in the area.

Our social life was extremely busy. Every night a long list posted on our bulletin board announced the squadron parties all over southern California to which we were invited. Each posting did its best to tempt us to attend that certain party.

Usually we could take our pick, but sometimes a bit of pressure was exerted to go to some special group's fling, especially on weekends. A notice might say, "You are invited to this party by order of the CO," and we would know that we'd better attend this party or have a very good excuse. Army, navy, or marine, these squadron parties were usually about the same: lots of food, drinks, music, and men, with very few women. We usually danced every dance, and we soon became adept at the fast comeback and joking required. Many parties had to be ignored because of our busy schedules. We felt guilty when this happened because we knew how important each was to the people involved.

Still, during the week there were a few free evenings and always plenty of dates available, with lots of evenings spent at the local nightclubs. We had all the party time we could stand.

San Diego was such fun! I remember trips to Tijuana, Mexico, to shop; watching the waves come in crested with shining phosphorous on dark enchanted nights in La Jolla; and enjoying the semitropical trees, flowers, and bushes, so different from Montana.

We still had to live by army rules, although in San Diego they were much more relaxed than in basic. No KP. No close-order drilling. However, someone decided we needed regular physical inspections, the female equivalent of the army's short-arms inspections. We realized the rationale, since we led such active social lives, but the methods used to perform this ritual were dehumanizing. Every few weeks, we were all ordered to lie on our beds minus skirts and underpants. An army doctor and a nurse proceeded down the line, giving each girl a quick vaginal inspection. And you may take my word for it that you felt like a piece of meat.

In silent objection, Martha, an older WAC, always doused her lower body before each of these inspections with liberal amounts of Tabu perfume. I wonder if any of the inspecting officers ever recognized the name of her perfume and realized Martha's secret contempt for them.

It would have taken only a few extra minutes to have performed these examinations in one of the noncom rooms at the end of the barracks to provide at least a bit of privacy and modesty. It was our opinion that some minor officer who hated the thought of women in the army and who considered us all whores was using this as a method of sexual harassment.

As far as I know, during these inspections nobody was ever discovered to be pregnant or to have any venereal disease. After several months, the inspections stopped. I was never subjected to this type of inspection before or after San Diego. I did meet male chauvinists everywhere in the army, usually dyed-in-the-wool army regulars who highly resented WACs. Still, most GIs treated us with respect and friendship and helped protect us from this prejudice against women.

After my traumatic experience with Claudia at Denton, I was much faster in recognizing the second lesbian I met in service. A small private room had been built at one end of the Balboa Park barracks for the noncom. Joan, the corporal in charge, roomed there. She was very mannish in appearance, lean, with short straight hair, and a deep voice. Although she was not so aggressive as Claudia had been, she did her best to entice one or another of the girls in the barracks to spend time in her room, but we all quietly agreed to leave her alone as much as possible, and I don't think she was able to find a playmate while we were there.

Life as a WAC in San Diego was more exciting than anything I had ever experienced. My job was rewarding and useful. My social life was tremendous. Being alive was wonderful.

However, all was not fun and games. We saw thousands of young men about to leave for the war in the Pacific, and a lot of servicemen who had just returned from the Pacific. They all needed someone to talk to, to laugh with, to dance with, to hold a little while so they could pretend that the world was all right. We had to learn to be fast on the repartee, but to listen when necessary. We couldn't let our sympathy show *too* much, because what they needed most was courage to forget some of their troubles and worries. I would often cry at night, remembering someone I had seen or talked to that day.

The young men just going out to war tried hard to put on a brave show, but underneath it was obvious that most of them were deeply afraid. Those who had just come back from the war tended to be quiet, morose, with sadness in their eyes. The big San Diego Naval Hospital was nearby, so we saw a lot of what the war had done to our men . . . lost arms, lost legs, ugly scars, twisted minds.

Thank goodness I never saw it, but friends told me of seeing combat nurses who had been captured by the enemy and later freed. They came back from the Pacific alive, but in boxes, with arms and legs missing, and with horribly mutilated bodies. We began to understand what *the horrors of war* really meant.

Special things seemed to keep happening to me. One day, three of us were chosen as part of an honor guard for launching a small ship. Dressed in Class A uniforms, we stood at attention through several speeches by dignitaries before the beribboned bottle was brought out and an admiral's wife performed the official christening. I hadn't realized before how hard it is to break a champagne bottle. It took four good swings before that bottle finally broke. Someone told us that failing to break the bottle on the first swing was considered a bad omen. I always worried about that ship.

Every Friday evening, a local middle-aged couple invited any service people who liked classical music to spend several hours listening to their fabulous library of classical records in their home high on a hill overlooking San Diego. Usually about a dozen servicepeople sat around on couches or cushions or on the floor, watching the sunset and the lights of the city far below as we listened to the greatest music of the world. There was very little conversation, just lots of music and plenty of snacks. Wonderful evenings. It was this couple's contribution to the morale of servicemen and servicewomen.

THREE MEN

There were a number of men in my life while I was stationed in San Diego, but I especially remember three of them . . . for three entirely different reasons.

My most special friend, Gerry, an air force noncom from New Jersey, was a talented musician and a very sweet, gentle person—and fun to be with. He made lots of spending money arranging music for many of the big-name bands, such as the Dorsey Brothers, Artie Shaw, Woody Herman, and others. Even with no piano available, he could arrange a piece of music for all the instruments in an entire orchestra. Gerry played a number of instruments well, especially the piano and trombone, and was a member of the Southern California Army Orchestra, which played for dances up and down the West Coast. Sometimes I traveled with Gerry and the orchestra to dance dates in southern California. Now and then during these evenings, Gerry would trade off with other musicians so we could dance. Gerry offered to make arrangements for me to sing with the group, but I was far too shy—and too unsure of my musical abilities—to try.

Whenever a name band came to the San Diego area to entertain the servicemen, Gerry usually knew either the leader or some of the musicians, and he introduced me to many of them: Tommy and Jimmy Dorsey, Stan Kenton, Artie Shaw, Les Brown, Bob Crosby, Woody Herman, and others.

I really liked Gerry, but I was essentially a ranch girl from Montana, and he embarrassed me to death. Everything was in the open with him, and he shouted to the world that he was in love. He didn't see why I couldn't understand his openness. I would blush from the roots of my hair to my heels and want to hide somewhere.

In October, on my birthday, we went to dinner at the fanciest restaurant in town, the El Coronado Hotel on an island in the bay. Our table had special candles and decorations, and when it was time for dessert, singing waiters brought in a big lighted cake. After the cake, they wheeled in a cart loaded with fancily wrapped presents that Gerry had bought for me with his music money—a watch, I remember, for one thing. There were even presents from his family back east, whom I had never met, and a lovely birthday card from his Uncle Bonaparte, the head of the family. This was all very sweet of Gerry, but far too flamboyant for my bashfulness. Instead of really appreciating it, my reaction was embarrassment. I wanted to sink under the table as other diners stared at us.

Every morning while we lived at the zoo, Gerry would meet me in the park and walk me to work. I could take either of two paths, so he found a low tree where he could sit in the lower branches to watch both trails. I got lots of teasing about all this.

Every evening Gerry waited for me after supper in our WAC day room. He would play a concert on the piano for everyone there until I arrived. Then, as I entered the room, he would break into "our song"—"I'll be loving you, always, / With a love that's true, always." This triumphal entry was just a bit too dramatic for a ranch girl from Montana.

Gerry wrote a lovely piece of music for me, "The Grace Concerto," which he told me the Philadelphia Symphony Orchestra had played in concert.

Gerry proposed a number of times, but I didn't think we could have had a successful marriage. Our temperaments and backgrounds were too different. He was married later, and after the war returned to New Jersey to lead an orchestra of his own on the East Coast.

Memories of another man in San Diego are not so pleasant. One evening I had a date to go to a movie with a GI from our headquarters. "George," from Chicago, was nice looking, well built, quiet—dull and boring. He had been asking me to go to a show with him for weeks, so one evening when Gerry was out of town, I agreed. We were walking downtown through the park past the tropical bird cages where the birds were making their usual sunset racket. George remarked that he had never stopped to see them, so we decided to walk through their arbor. No one was around, and as soon as we entered the secluded area, George started to attack me. We were having quite a wrestling match on one of the benches until I got really angry and yelled "Stop it, you rat!"

As abruptly as he had started the attack, he quit. He was shaking, almost crying. "Please, don't call me that. I'm sorry. Just don't ever call me that!"

"Well, okay," I said, "but let's get out of here."

He looked at me a second, then, a bit more slowly than at first but just as wildly, began to attack me again. He was so strong that I knew rape was unavoidable.

"You dirty rat!" I shouted. "Leave me alone! You really *are* a rat!"

And immediately he let me go again. This time he was really crying as he begged me not to call him that awful name. I headed for the exit as fast as I could with him following, begging my forgiveness all the way.

The office building where we worked was about a block away, so I ran there, knowing there would be a guard on duty at the front desk. Luckily, the GI on duty was a friend of mine. He evidently knew "George," too. No questions were asked. "George" was invited to leave, and a cab was called to take me back to the barracks.

I never figured out the magic in the word *rat*, except that he was from the slums of Chicago and had obviously had a traumatic experience involving rats. The other headquarters personnel saw to it that I had no further contact with the man.

That was the closest I have ever come to being raped, and it was frightening.

One night a curious thing happened to me.

The scene: an old theater in downtown San Diego.

The time: an evening in early 1944.

The characters: my WAC company, various other military personnel, and several army battalions slated for departure the next morning for the Pacific war zone where fighting was at the peak.

Two of my friends and I sat at the left side of the theater toward the front to avoid the main crowd. We were not looking forward to several hours of army training films about subjects such as loose lips sink ships, buy war bonds, and articles of war, but it was a requirement. We had been bused downtown for the event and were ordered to take the same bus back to the barracks when it was over. No exceptions! That was an order!

As the film started, we heard the row behind us fill up. It was a group of young officers from one of the companies sailing in the morning. There was the usual banter and light flirting until some WAC officer yelled for silence and things quieted down.

Despite the warning, the officer sitting behind me kept whispering in my ear.

"Where ya from, corporal?"

"Iowa."

"Been in San Diego long?"

"About six months."

"Have a boyfriend?"

"Lots of them."

"What did you do before you joined the army?"

"Taught grade school in Iowa. Hey, we're supposed to be quiet."

"Mind if I join you?" And he was up and over the seat and sitting beside me in the seat next to the wall.

In the next half hour he told me a little about himself. He was very charming, handsome, and intelligent, a graduate of a good midwestern university, obvious family money. He liked the army most of the time and was proud of his artillery unit. He also told me of the things he had wanted in his life and that now he was afraid he would never be able to do or to get. His greatest regrets were that he had never married or had children.

We got shushed again, so he sat for a while with his arm around me, just looking at me. "Why don't we take off out of here and have something to eat or drink?"

"I'm supposed to stay with my company tonight. Orders."

"But I'm sailing in the morning!"

"I wish I could, but I can't. Really."

"Will you marry me tonight?"

"Wha-a-at?"

"Please," he said with sudden urgency. "Say yes. Please! I don't have anyone to come home to . . . and I have a feeling inside that if I don't have someone waiting for me, I'll never come home." A reluctant tear squeezed out of the corner of his eye as he put his head on my shoulder to hide his face. This wasn't kidding or pretending, and it wasn't funny at all . . . just suddenly, overwhelmingly sad.

"But you have your family and friends," I gulped.

"But there is no one special waiting for me. . . and I *need* someone." He was begging now. "You don't have to sleep with me . . . just marry me tonight. You'll get my army allowance, and I'll sign my insurance all over to you. Everything. Just be Mrs. Kent Davis." His hands shook, and his face was contorted with his sincerity and need. "I can't go without anyone to remember or hold onto or write to. I'll never find my way back again if no one cares."

"But we couldn't get married so quickly. And I'd be AWOL. And you don't know what kind of person I really am."

"I'll find a way to get married. It's been done before. And you can straighten things out with your sarge tomorrow. It'll be okay. And I know already that I like you. We can get better acquainted with letters . . . please write me now and then . . . and after the war if you *really* don't like me, you can have a divorce. Just marry me tonight before I go . . . please. Please!"

The temptation was strong. My heart bled for him. By this time I was in tears too. "But I just *can't*," I whispered. "Marriage should be more than this."

"But I don't have *time* to make it more. I *promise* I'll make it up to you later. I promise!! Please let there be a Mrs. Kent Davis so I'll leave someone of my own behind when I'm dead."

Suddenly the film ended. The lights snapped on, and the WAC sergeant bawled, "All WACs line up at the side entrance for the bus. Immediately!"

I stood up with the rest. As I looked back at him I whispered, "I'm sorry. I'm *so* sorry." He was crying openly.

How could the despair of that night be forgotten? It was a fact that many men had a feeling before they went overseas that they would never come home again. In most cases, they say that the ones who felt this premonition really did not come back. I have often wondered if Kent made it, and I have said many prayers for him. I wonder if I should have gone AWOL that night, and what difference it would have made in my life— or his.

I was a typical, wholesome-looking American girl, so I received several dozen proposals during the war. Some were frivolous, spur-of-the-moment ideas. Some were very serious. But none of them bothered me as much as the one from Lieutenant Davis.

HOW LUCKY CAN YOU GET?

One day in August, our bulletin board at Quetzal Hall in San Diego carried a notice: "All WAC personnel interested in volunteering for an overseas assignment sign your name and serial number below."

Without knowing where we might be heading, or when, almost everyone in the company signed.

This notice was nearly forgotten until one day several weeks later when word came back from the upper echelons that two girls from our company had been chosen to go to England as part of a special group to join the first small group of WACs already over there. And I was one of them!

Before the date set to report at Fort Oglethorpe in northern Georgia, Sally and I were given two weeks leave in late November to go home and tell our families good-bye. We would miss Christmas at home, but at least we would get to visit our homes and families before going abroad.

Passenger services in the United States had been second-rated to wartime freight handling. Most trains were filled to capacity with troops and war supplies, so we were lucky to find any way to get home. In San Diego, I boarded a train for St. Louis. I had to sit on my duffel bag most of the way because it was so crowded. From St. Louis, the only way I could get to Iowa was by a train known locally as the jitney. This last part of the trip was exasperatingly slow because we were either hailed down, or someone stepped off, at every crossroads and hamlet. The old train, which had been pressed back in service to ease transportation problems, included an old-time steam engine, six or seven boxcars, and one passenger car. The small group of passengers sat on straight-backed hard seats, all facing front, with a wood stove in one of the front corners of the car to keep us warm. An ancient conductor stoked the heating stove now and then from a pile of logs and a coal scuttle in the corner. If we opened a window, we were smothered with black, sooty smoke from the engine; if we kept the windows closed, we choked on smoke from the wood and coal heater. When I finally got off at Cedar Rapids, I was exhausted. My back ached, and I was covered with soot and dust. The cold Midwest was a far cry from jasmine-scented San Diego. Nevertheless, I felt very lucky to get home.

My one week at home, all that was left after travel time, went by much too swiftly. My family and I spent every minute together, but we had no dramatic good-bye scene. I think we were all afraid to get too sentimental for fear that showing too much worry and fear might make things harder for each other. I was leaving for the European war zone. That was that. We had to accept it, and God willing, I would come home again soon.

After my leave I reported to Fort Oglethorpe for several weeks of preparation for overseas duty. There were more training films—*Loose Lips Sink Ships* (again the film about security), *Sad Sack with Rubber Gloves* (a film on VD where poor Sad Sack, the epitome of a new recruit, sees so many VD films that he insists on donning rubber gloves when introduced to a girl)—as well as lectures on army rules and the use of gas masks. And there was lots of PE, rifle practice, and target shooting. (I became adept at breaking down and cleaning a Lee-Enfield army rifle.) As a ranch girl, I was already used to guns, so I scored high at target practice. I was not fast, but look out, Nazis!

Speaking of shots, there were also lots of the other type of shots, usually administered in a long double line: GIs on one side, WACs on the other. One six-foot, handsome specimen of a man passed out cold in front of me after his third immunization shot in a row; he was much chagrined when he came to.

Our duffel bags were crammed tight with all the things the Fort Oglethorpe officers had heard were in short supply in England: soap, toilet paper, and Kotex. (Of course, after lugging pounds of these things across the Atlantic, we found them easily available and in good supply in the United Kingdom.) Our duffel bags and backpacks were packed and repacked. Even our extra shoes were jammed full of underwear or toilet paper to save space. Almost all personal items had to be abandoned. Those packed duffels felt as though they weighed a ton. We had to lug them everywhere we went. That meant dragging those millstones through long lines onto troop trains, onto ships, across miles of camps. It didn't take much persuasion to leave behind anything the army did not absolutely require.

Each of us was issued new olive drab wool winter uniforms, light khaki cotton summer uniforms, green and white seersucker fatigues (or work dresses), and sufficient khaki-colored underwear and stockings to last at least a year. (Were they *really* khaki-colored? Yes! That's a question everyone wants answered—just as everyone is curious about what Scotsmen wear under those kilts.) Overshoes, "Lil' Abner" boots (high-topped laced boots that rubbed our ankles sore), raincoats, helmets, mess kits, even olive drab gas masks had to be stuffed into our gear somewhere. Someone had even remembered to issue us sewing kits with khaki-colored thread and buttons. Hooray for army efficiency! Some joker started the crazy rumor that we would be issued khaki-colored toothpicks soon. We all laughed because we were sure that no room could be found in those bags for even one toothpick.

Our stay at Fort Oglethorpe was prolonged an extra week until space was available for us on a troopship. We marked time with "hurry up and wait" lines, more films and lectures, KP, and checking our gear. Finally, we boarded a train to Camp Shanks, New York, a particularly damp, cold, soggy, dour, unpleasant place. The train ride through the Appalachians and the Washington, D.C., slums had been interesting but fairly unpleasant, and Camp Shanks was awful. We were grateful that we only had to spend a week in that hellhole.

At Camp Shanks we learned how to board a ship by climbing up a cargo net hung over the side and to disembark the same way. This skill was practiced in full battle dress: helmets and helmet liner, wool Eisenhower jacket, cotton shirt, wool slacks, "Lil' Abner" boots, and wool socks, carrying a full back-pack, a mess kit, and our stuffed duffels. At least we did not have to carry weapons and ammunition.

Our practice ship kept rolling back and forth against the dock, and I just knew I was going to be smashed flat between the dock and the ship at any moment or be pulled over backward by the weight on my back. I survived, of course. And, of course, it never again became necessary to know how to use this precarious ability.

COLD KIDNEY STEW

Forty young women of the United States Women's Army Corps in full battle dress including helmets, carrying all their gear, marched up the gangplank of the *Queen Mary* that cold morning of February 12, 1944.

We were thrilled at the thought of sailing on such a luxurious ocean liner. We were going to England first class, even though this huge ship had lost her bright peacetime colors and was now repainted a dirty, rust-streaked, green-gray camouflage color.

We were also pleased (and relieved) to find that we could walk aboard the ship via the gangplank rather than climbing up over the side on cargo nets.

The forty WACs were the only women on board. Our quarters were deep inside the ship, well-guarded from the thousands of male GIs aboard. We were allowed on deck now and then and managed to see most of the ship in spite of our guards. Our cabins would have been very comfortable for one or two persons instead of the eight or ten assigned to each. There were tiers of bunks three high on either side of the small rooms. We tried to spend as much time as possible outside of the cabin because of the crowding and because of our seasick roommates.

Some friendly GIs slipped us cookies through the gate at the end of our passageway, advising us to keep something in our stomachs so we would not get seasick. I'm not sure if it was that advice and the cookies or the idea that I, a Montana girl who had ridden some rough horses in my day, was not going to let this ride get to me, but I did not get seasick. Some of the girls, and many of the men as well, became ill while we were still anchored in the choppy New York harbor. They spent a horrible week at sea before we got to England.

Many other girls became deathly ill at our first breakfast aboard ship. Every inch of the *Queen Mary* had been converted to wartime use for transporting as many troops as possible. The WACs were assigned to a mess set up in a former swimming pool on one of the lower decks. The Italian tile walls were still there, but long wooden tables filled the windowless room with benches on either side of the tables. The ship was manned by a British crew, so we were in for a week of English chow.

No one who was there will ever forget that first breakfast! The ship was beginning to roll in the rough waters just outside New York harbor, so the big tin dishpans full of food at each table slid slowly back and forth, back and forth, back and forth, from one end of the table to the other end. English stewards stood at the aisle end of each table, trying to catch the pans before they could spill onto the floor. Just the sight of that slow back and forth motion sent some of the girls scurrying out of the room, their faces a peculiar shade of green.

Those who were a little braver peeked at the food in the big round dishpans . . . and a few more left hurriedly. The menu consisted of cold, gray, thick slices of bread heavily smeared with tasteless white margarine; cold, greasy, grayish kidney stew; cold hard-boiled eggs in the shell; and tin pitchers of barely lukewarm aged tea, gray with canned milk. In the heavy seas, the dishpanfuls of this awful food went back and forth, back and forth.

Most of us who could force ourselves to eat at least a little of this stuff managed to keep from being sick, but the English sure saved a lot of money on food during that voyage by serving that breakfast.

Our trip across the North Atlantic was stormy. In winter, that infamous ocean has some of the roughest seas in the world. During the war, the *Queen Mary* traveled without an escort because she could go faster alone. To keep submarines from having time to get a bearing to fire their torpedoes, she changed course every few minutes. This zigzagging made for very rough riding and added several days to the trip. We were not required to have more than one boat drill or to wear life jackets, although these were always readily available. We asked an English deck hand one day if we were in danger of being attacked. "Not bloody likely," he answered. "Safest ship afloat."

We tried to keep our food down and our spirits up. Our favorite joke on the trip was about the officer who was reaming out an enlisted man aboard ship: "If you call the deck a floor one more time, I'll throw you out that little round window over there!"

Going up on deck was a great treat after our crowded cabins. We took pleasure just watching the seabirds against the gray clouds and high waves. Sometimes on the horizon we saw convoys of ships and their air cover and heard the ships' horns greeting each other or watched their signal lights. Then fog would descend and these ships would seem unreal, like quiet, gray ghosts gliding across the water.

About halfway through the voyage, we had that brush with the German submarine, and we began to realize that we were really in a war zone.

The white cliffs of Dover were a welcome sight, even on that stormy, gray, windy day a week and a half later when we sailed into the English Channel. We had arrived in England! We were now in the ETO (European theater of operations) to help the Allied forces prepare for D-day—if we could only survive the German attacks until then.

2

ENGLAND

BUSHEY, HERTS

Had I been older or wiser, I would have been extremely nervous about going to England in 1943. The London area was being bombed day and night by the Germans, and there was always the fear that they would attempt an invasion of England at any time. But I was young, convinced that nothing could get past the invisible shield that protected me. That feeling of invincibility in young people keeps armies in business.

After the *Queen Mary* docked in Bournemouth in southern England, we were processed through the debarkation center and hustled off to London by train.

In spite of the familiar language around us, the small English railroad cars, with aisles down one side and a series of roomettes down the other side, convinced us we were now in a foreign country. These little trains had big round bumpers between the cars, shrill whistles, doors on one side of each roomette to the outside, and doors on the other side to the corridors running the length of the cars. Although they always smelled of coal smoke, they were clean, efficient, and fairly comfortable.

Having been raised with lots of open space, clear skies, miles and miles between things, and magnificent views of prairies or faraway mountains, my first impression of England was that it was like a doll's house. Every little piece of the landscape was so manicured, so well-cared-for, and so fully used. It was lovely, with gorgeous trees and bushes, ponds and streams, but everything was so *close*. Fogs and humidity restricted the views to the next hedgerow or two, only a few hundred feet away. At first I felt hemmed in and claustrophobic, but gradually I became used to things being closer and began to enjoy the real beauty and placidity of the English countryside.

In London we were divided into small groups and sent on to our assigned stations. Four or five of us went to the Eighth Air Force headquarters in Bushey, Hertfordshire, about twenty miles northwest of London, to join a small group of WACs already there.

The Bushey, Herts (pronounced "Hearts"), HQ was set up on a country estate leased to the U.S. Army Air Force for the duration. The surrounding countryside was green—full of trees, hedges, stone fences, grass, and flowers. Small bands of sheep performed the tasks of mowing the grass and keeping the meadows and hillsides neat. Close by was the old town of Bushey with an underground railroad station on a direct line to London.

About forty WACs occupied two barracks and an office-dayroom complex in a meadow about a block from the small "castle" (we called it a castle, though it was more like a manor house) where the HQ offices were housed. We were fascinated with the old stone castle's courtyards, ballrooms, endless corridors, gorgeous woodwork, and ornate decorations. The GIs who had helped set up the HQ told grisly tales of rats as big as cats living in the basements and walls, but I never saw one—and never went looking for them.

It was a pleasure to use the bathrooms in the HQ building. They had WCs (water closets) with pull chains like almost all English loos. But these facilities had lovely hand-painted flowers inside the washbasins as well as inside and outside of the toilet bowls. We almost felt guilty using all those painted cabbage roses for such common purposes.

One question about this castle was never solved for us. At the topmost peak of the highest tower was a heavy metal hook about four feet high. The only possible reason for such a sky-hook we could dream up was to anchor a dirigible, although it looked far too ancient for that, so it remained a mystery to us. "Maybe it's to fasten on to a cloud to hold the whole castle up," one girl laughed.

Army life in wartime England was vastly different from army life in the States, but certain rules and regulations still had to be enforced. There was bed check at 2300 hours. We still pulled occasional KP. Full uniforms were worn at all times, including ties—and especially dog tags.

However, barracks inspections were now cursory. Sometimes we were not even there—the sergeant just walked through and left notes on the bulletin board in the dayroom, if necessary. We still had cleaning duties around our barracks and grounds, of course, but pressures about "spit and polish" inspections were much more relaxed than in the States.

KP duty had to be endured, but did not come often, and we did not have to do the really grubby work such as cleaning grease traps. I was especially lucky because the sergeant in charge of the dining hall, a handsome, quiet Irishman from Iowa, made sure I was never assigned the worst KP jobs like cleaning out the dozens of ash trays. I didn't smoke, so he thought that it was not right to make me do this stinky job. We soon became friends, and he became my protector while I was on KP, which I appreciated. So I really did have it easy.

I had never smoked, so with cigarettes and chocolates strictly rationed, I was glad to trade my cigarettes to the heavier smokers among my friends for candy bars. Sometimes when things got especially tense I would feel a real desire to smoke, but there was always someone around who needed nicotine even more, so I continued to be a nonsmoker.

WACs held interesting and responsible jobs in the Eighth Air Force. Most of us worked at the castle as secretaries or in specialty jobs. Mary and I were cryptographers. Helen and Verna were court reporters. All of us had been carefully selected for our work, much of which was classified, but since all of us had sat through endless lectures and training films about keeping all information about our jobs secret, there was no shop talk, even in the barracks.

Our first sergeant was a six-foot, no-nonsense, very dignified woman named Sergeant Reddy. She was marvelous at her job. Sergeant Reddy was eminently fair, unflappable, understanding, and stern, and we all loved and respected her. I can't remember any griping or complaints about her rules and discipline. A girl who broke a rule got extra cleaning or KP, or lost some leave time. We appreciated our relative freedom from unnecessarily strict army rules and tried not to abuse our privileges. I knew of only one girl who had to be sent home from England, and we never were told why. She may have been pregnant, or maybe the bombings got to her, but the sergeant made sure that nothing leaked out about the matter. The girl just quietly left for home one day.

Gasoline, or petrol as it is called in England, was for military use only, so bicycles, trains, and buses were the only ways to travel. Everyone understood this, and there was little complaint. Then one day Sergeant Reddy announced, "Anyone who wishes to go biking may now check a bicycle out at the company dayroom." Sure enough, a dozen old English bikes were lined up outside the door for us to use during our time off. We had noticed large numbers of bikes on the narrow, tree-lined English lanes and roads, and had been amused by the riders: groups of children peddling merrily along in school uniforms and caps, books strapped on their backs; plump housewives hurrying to buy their daily rations of food at the various small shops; businessmen sitting bolt upright, dressed in business suits, ties, and bowler hats, briefcases tucked under their arms, looking neither right nor left; older men and women headed at a slower pace for the grocers or on errands; all looking totally proper and stiff as they pedaled busily along, dodging pedestrians, occasional cars, bomb rubble, and small dogs with equal disdain and equanimity.

Now we could join this club. Although we enjoyed this recreation very much, we never did reach the English level of dignity and imperturbability on a bike. After we got used to the idea of cars being on the left side of the road, we found that biking was the best way to see the countryside. My friends and I spent as much free time as possible peddling down narrow lanes and finding hidden villages with thatched roofs and Elizabethan cottages of timber and plaster, isolated neighborhood pubs, little-known historical spots, old mazes, forgotten castles and gardens, and ancient churches. The people we met on these excursions, amazed to see American girls so far afield, always treated us with utmost courtesy and friendliness. Many of the out-of-the-way hamlets were like picture postcards.

We would often have a bite to eat at the local pubs where few Americans were ever seen. Often, someone would insist we have an "'arf 'n 'arf" with them, and then "'ave a go" at a game of darts. They always won, of course, but we got better at the game as time went by, and it helped us make a lot of friends.

On our bike trips, we learned a lot about the local history of the middle English countryside and its people. We saw first-hand the cost of the war to ordinary English citizens and heard some sad tales. We also answered a lot of questions about the United States and our home. Invariably someone had a cousin in Milwaukee or a brother in Denver or Miami whom they hoped we knew. It was as hard for them to realize how big our country is as it was for us to get used to their smaller spaces.

Hertfordshire is in the heartland of England between two low groups of hills, the Cotswolds and the Chilterns. The heartlands include Bucks (Buckinghamshire), Herts (Hertfordshire), Oxon (Oxfordshire), Berks (Berkshire), Beds (Bedfordshire), Glos (Gloucestershire), and Warwick (Warwickshire).

Herts had the distinction of being the only place where churches had snuffers, which are small rectangular towers topped with tiny spires.

All through the area were many ancient houses and shops with steep tiled roofs and tall gables. Most of the towns were very small market towns with numerous little shops to serve the needs of the local people. Our general impression of the area was of a very pleasant, quiet, well-bred, and genteel garden spot with beautiful old mansions and gardens and picturesque villages along the one-lane country roads.

Our barracks at Bushey was fairly comfortable but cold. Each barracks had a wood stove in the middle of the floor, but fuel was scarce. With the prevalent fog and rain, the stoves were a poor match for the ever-present dampness and cold. We dressed warmly during the days. At night we bundled up in our flannel pajamas and piled on as many wool blankets as we could get hold of.

The cold seemed to bother Verna most of all. Each night she would spend fifteen minutes getting dressed for bed: flannel pajamas, sweatshirt, flannel robe, woolen socks, wool shirt, woolen knit fatigue hat pulled down over her ears, and on really cold nights, woolen scarf and mittens. Plus a pile of woolen blankets. Then she would lie there, teeth chattering, complaining about how cold her dog tags were on her chest, until she warmed up enough to go to sleep. She vowed that after she got out of the army she would live the rest of her life in a hot climate and never be cold again.

The wet English winter weather had an embarrassing effect on many WACs—difficulty in maintaining bladder control. It was so embarrassing for a girl to be kissing her boyfriend good night after a long evening at the pub! Her friend would not understand why she suddenly broke off a passionate kiss and dashed madly for the barracks, but too much beer, and all that dripping rain, were a combination not to be denied.

My own problem was that I was tired a lot of the time, partly because of the weather and my odd working hours and partly as a result of my busy social life. As soon as I returned to the barracks, no matter what time of day or night, I would lie down on my bunk to rest. Soon my barracks nickname became "Horizontal." A few minutes at rest, though, and I was ready to go again.

All mail from the European theater of operation had to be written on V-mail forms, small sheets of lightweight paper. Everything we wrote had to be censored before it left the area, but letters from home were not censored and were always extremely welcome. During World War I, mail had often taken many months each way, but our mail went through quickly. Packages from home arrived in good shape and usually within one month from when they were mailed. We thought this was pretty reasonable, considering that it was wartime. Our mothers sent us regular shipments of cookies and other goodies, and the arrival of a box from home excited everyone—because we always shared any edible contents.

As in the States, we were invited to a number of company parties and dances. Of necessity, these were not as elaborate as the parties had been stateside, but we made a lot of new friends and had as full a social life as we could stand.

One such party ended in an ugly way for me—through my own carelessness. A group of WACs were guests at a company dance held at a small country club in an isolated spot ten or fifteen miles from our headquarters. We were driven over in an army truck, which was to call for us afterward. The dancing area was crowded and hot and the band was poor and loud.

"This place is getting me down. Too much noise. Too much smoke. And it's hot," I complained to Joe, the GI I was dancing with. I had known Joe for some time and liked him, so when he suggested we go outside on the porch for some air, I agreed.

The moon was shining on the small lake beside the club-house and it was a lovely night. "Let's take a walk around the lake," Joe suggested, and off we went on the footpath skirting the edge of the water. We ambled happily along, enjoying the mild breeze, talking about home and company gossip. Then, when we were about two-thirds of the way around the lake, our conversation ended abruptly as we realized that the faint music from across the lake was the last song of the night, "Good Night, Ladies."

"Whoops, the dance is breaking up," Joe said. "Better run for it."

Off we dashed, but not fast enough. By the time we reached the clubhouse, the WAC truck was gone. I was horrified. Here I was, in the middle of nowhere—no buses or trains—miles from headquarters.

"What will I do? How in the world will I ever get back to Bushey?" I gasped in panic. We were in the middle of the coun-tryside, in the middle of the night, with nobody around, and I had no idea which country lanes to take even if I tried walk-ing back to camp.

"I'll see if you can catch a ride in our company's truck," my friend said. "We have to drive right past your compound any-way."

The truck driver reluctantly agreed, and I piled into the back of the truck with twenty or more half-drunk GIs I didn't know, but Joe squeezed me in on one of the benches between himself and his friend Paul. It was dark under the canvas top, but in the flashes of matches lighting cigarettes I could see that the bench on the other side of the truck was jammed with GIs. And lying across their laps was a very drunk English girl. As we jounced down the country lanes, her giggling and squealing had the attention of every GI in the truck.

"I'm getting scared," I whispered in Joe's ear.

"Just don't say anything," he whispered back. "Paul and I will take care of you, but *be quiet.*"

Things got pretty out of hand in that girl's part of the truck, and soon hands started grabbing at me in the dark from every angle, mussing my hair, feeling my legs, whatever they could touch. Silently, desperately, Joe, Paul, and I fended them off. Nothing was said. Everyone was too busy listening to the squeals and giggles on the opposite bench. Just hands everywhere.

I thought that truck would never get to Bushey. When at last we arrived at our gate, the guards watched in surprise as one very frightened, very disheveled WAC came tumbling down at top speed from the back of the truck, with male voices calling after her, "Aw, honey, don't go—we've got the rest of the night to party" and "Come on, let's have some fun, we haven't got acquainted yet."

"I missed the WAC truck back," I gasped. The two guards knew me. They said nothing except "Pass, corporal," and let me dash to the safety of the WAC area. I was never so glad to get home in my life.

Nothing was ever mentioned again about this incident. But whenever we went to a party after that I made sure I was the first one on the return truck. And for a while I had bad dreams about hands grabbing at me.

LOVE IN THE ETO

American GIs were homesick, so American girls looked and sounded awfully good to them. We were invited to a great many company parties, but work schedules kept us from attending most of them. Dates were easily available to all of us if we had time for them.

Enlisted WACs were not supposed to date officers, but the rule was never enforced. One army captain from a unit in northern England came to London quite often to see me. Charles and I ate in all the best restaurants, attended all the best plays and parties, and met many officers from our units, and nothing was ever said to either of us about our enlisted-officer relationship.

Surprisingly, there was little dating between our company of WACs and the GIs in our HQ. Perhaps this was because these GIs usually treated us like kid sisters. They were very protective, especially if someone made any derogatory remarks about us.

Take one ugly scene in Bushey as an example. Verna and I were walking down to the Bushey station to catch the underground into London when we walked past several American soldiers. Their insignia showed they were from a unit stationed in eastern England and were apparently on leave. Also, they had obviously been enjoying a number of brews in local pubs.

"Hey, look! WACs!" one of them yelled. "Where ya goin'? Come have a drink with us and be friendly."

We greeted them politely and explained that we had a train to catch.

"Aw, ya just can't bother with GIs, that's all," one of them sneered. "Yer just damn officers' whores. Too stuck up to get friendly with us plain GIs, ain'tcha." And he grabbed my arm and started to pull me backward.

Some enlisted men from our HQ walking down a nearby street heard the loud voices and saw what was going on. They ran across the street, pushed the drunks away from us, and stood glaring at them as they said, "Look, you! These are darn nice girls and you'd better treat them like ladies or you'll have us to fight. Now, get out of here! And clean your mouths up!"

The drunks backed off, grumbling, "Ah, if yer goin' ta make such an issue about it, okay." But they wasted no time getting out of there.

"Thanks, guys. You're real friends in need," we said. "We sure appreciate your help."

"Ah, that's okay, girls. Any time. See you around." And off we went on our separate ways.

Shortly after we arrived in Bushey, one of my friend Helen's special friends, a very pretty, sweet girl from Ohio named

Sharon, met Robert, a handsome air force staff sergeant, at a company dance. They fell madly in love. After months of filling out army forms and English questionnaires, arrangements were finally made for them to be married in the company dayroom at Robert's base northeast of London. Helen, four other girls, and I were invited to the small wedding and given permission by our C.O. to travel to that base.

The room was a regular army day room with a few paper garlands here and there. The bride and groom and the chaplain were all in regular dress uniforms. It was a gloomy day, an uninspiring setting, no fancy wedding outfits—just a small corsage of roses for the bride to carry. But the glow on the bride's face matched the glow on the groom's face, and together they lighted up the whole room. They had eyes only for each other, and no one could miss the fact that they really, truly loved each other. It was the happiest, most romantic wedding I have ever attended.

Another wedding almost didn't happen. Jack, a sergeant at our headquarters, fell in love with a pretty English girl from Bushey. Plans were made for a big church wedding and all the necessary permission slips had been obtained from the U.S. Army, the British government, and the Church of England.

The girl's family was not well-off, so Jack promised to pay for a proper wedding and honeymoon. He had saved enough money for the wedding and for his bride's ticket to the United States after the war as well as for magnificent diamond engagement and wedding rings. But Jack was caught up in a group of noncoms who held big poker games every payday night, and he was on a losing streak.

Suddenly he realized that the wedding money was all gone. In desperation, he asked his fiancée to pawn the rings. With that cash, he was sure he could win all his money back. But he lost again.

A wireless message requesting money was sent to his family

in the States, but the money they sent was gambled away before it even arrived.

The girl canceled the church wedding plans, and Jack's friends in his company paid for a cheap wedding ring and a wedding lunch of fish 'n chips after the couple was married by an army chaplain (for free).

THE ENGLISH AND THE AMERICANS

"Don't use the word *bloody* over here," warned Sergeant Reddy. "It's considered a very bad swear word." Indeed it was! Each time "bloody" was heard, all proper English women—and even some men—would gasp and look horrified.

Certain English phrases tickled our fancy: "That's a sticky wicket," "Well blimey, mite, whatcher doin'?" "Lor' luv a duck!" "Harya this mornin', ducky?" "Whatta toff," "Ta ta for now," or just "Ta" (meaning "thanks").

We thought we all spoke basic English, but the American vocabulary and usage differed a great deal from the language used in England. Soon we knew what lorries, lifts, loos, and petrol were, but it took longer to understand some of the various British accents. Each section of London, every small area of the countryside, and even each school, had its own style of speech, some difficult to understand until you got used to them.

We all knew that "bobbies" were policemen, but we didn't know a "surgery" was a doctor's office, or that "the chemist's" was a drugstore. Now we found out that a "torch" was a flashlight. Men wore "braces" (suspenders), "jumpers" (pullover sweaters), "plus-fours" (baggy trousers), vests (undershirts), and waistcoats (vests), and carried "brollies" (umbrellas). Babies wore "nappies" (diapers) and rode in "prams" (baby carriages). Ladies wore "suspenders" (garters) and "plimsolls" (sneakers).

"Lorries" (trucks), "charabancs" (sight-seeing buses), and "saloon cars" (sedans) did not "yield" at corners, but "gave way." "Roundabouts" were traffic circles. "Priorities" were traffic right-of-ways.

"Trunk calls" (long distance calls) were made from "kiosks" (phone booths) if you wanted to "ring up" somebody (call them). People lived in "flats" (apartments) and used "flannels" (washcloths) in their "lavatories" (bathrooms). They smoked "fags" (cigarettes) and used "sticking plaster" (band-aids) and "rubbers" (erasers). They "queued up" (lined up) with "shopping trolleys" (shopping carts) to buy "tins" (cans of food). And their "quids" (pounds) went too fast, especially if they were "redundant" (out of work) after an air raid.

And on and on, from "nought" (zero) to "zed" (the letter z) until we were quite "daft," "bonkers," or "crackers" (mildly insane or confused).

People ate tea or high tea (a light supper) about five in the afternoon and enjoyed "toad-in-the-hole" (sausages baked in a Yorkshire pudding), and they even liked "swedes" (rutabagas), "broad beans" (limas), and "pasties" (meat turnovers). Desserts included "squashed flies" (raisin cookies), "Swiss rolls" (jelly rolls), "squash" (a fruit-flavored drink), or "jelly" (Jello).

The English money system was another problem at first, but we soon became adept at using pounds, shillings, and ha'pennies (and even at counting our change).

Even the English billboards were different from those at home. It was months before I knew what Bovril was, although numerous big advertising signs extolled its virtues: "Bovril, best for pregnant women," "Bovril, best for nursing mothers," "Bovril, best for growing children," and so forth. It became a standing joke among us to dream up other "Best for's," the cornier the better: "Best for hangovers," "Best for lovers," "Best for tired dogs," "Best for unfriendly ants," "Best for sick giraffes." (Yes, we did try the stuff later and decided our American bouillon was similar but not as rank.)

How we yearned for a good American hamburger and a Coke! Evenings in the barracks inevitably resulted in conversations about American foods, or about how good Mom's pot roast or chocolate cake or oatmeal cookies were.

Before long, somebody would volunteer to go for fish 'n chips, which were never rationed. Everyone would donate a few pence for the treat, and off we would go half a mile to the nearest fish 'n chips stand. Wrapped in sheets of old newspaper, the chips— French fries—were always hot and delicious, and the hot slices of fish were crisp and tasty. When we were hungry enough, they were a pretty fair substitute for hamburgers.

Much English food was not as good as fish 'n chips. Eating in most English restaurants was not much of a pleasure. Wartime shortages had drastically cut the supplies of fruit, vegetables, sugar, and meat, and the English penchant for boiling all foods for long periods didn't help. Not much talent or imagination was evident in the preparation of what was available. Very little seasoning was used on anything. Meals were bland, heavy, and uninteresting. Lots of Yorkshire puddings (which can be good, but were often just soggy and heavy) and stews (some good, some awful). Desserts were best because English people love sweets, and even with wartime sugar rationing it was sometimes possible to find "biscuits" (cookies) or "trifles." English trifles are lovely: bits of sponge cake, vanilla pudding, fruits, wine, all beautifully arranged and delicious.

Once in a while we discovered some very good restaurants. One place where we enjoyed eating was an Italian restaurant in London. Careful cooking and seasoning made the available food edible. They even managed to have a very decent dessert cart. And the proprietor, Luigi, a huge old Italian man, made it a point to greet all his guests personally. He was always particularly cordial to my friends and me: "Ah, zee Americain ladeez! I loff you! Come in, come in. Welcome! The best in the house for you." We would each receive a crushing hug and a kiss on both cheeks. We would be given the best table and the best service in the place.

As we left, Luigi would kiss our hands and urge us to come back to honor his restaurant again soon. We would float off down the street, forgetting the grimness around us for a while in the warm glow of the wonderful meal and Luigi's friendly welcome.

MISS HARRISON

Though most local English people were polite, helpful, and easy to talk with, only a few accepted us as real friends whom they would invite into their homes. One of these was a sweet, cultured, middle-aged ex-teacher named Miss Harrison. I never knew her given name, but "Miss Harrison" was all that was necessary. Anything more familiar would have seemed undignified. She lived in a pleasant flat in central Bushey with another elderly lady who never seemed to have much to say, but who smiled at us a lot.

Miss Harrison had great sympathy for "these poor young American girls so far from home." She did her best to show her friendship and appreciation for our country's help in the war. Although the English were strictly rationed on almost all food items, somehow Miss Harrison squeezed out enough from her meager allowance of food to provide a tea for us every Friday. Usually three or four of us would be invited to enjoy hot tea and dainty sandwiches served in front of her fireplace. Several little streams meandering through Bushey were filled with watercress, and the town bragged of being the "Watercress Capital of the World." Crisp and fresh, watercress leaves were used with thinly buttered, thinly sliced bread to make delicious small tea sandwiches. We often brought treats from home or American candy bars, which the two ladies cut in dainty pieces for all of us to enjoy. Once in a while, for a special treat, we would have a cracker or two. English crackers are what we call cookies.

At Christmas, Miss Harrison invited several of us for a holiday dinner. She must have saved her food coupons for months! We had real roast beef, practically nonexistent in England at that time, and Yorkshire pudding. For dessert she had made a real cake, which must have used up half a year's ration of sugar. The cake was decorated with white icing and a small winter scene with tiny china figurines, a tiny mirror lake, and a colored frosting landscape. Each of us received one of the figurines as a souvenir of the day and of our friendship. After dinner, we sat before her fireplace a long time, missing our families and Christmas at home, but consoled by the sincere friendliness and concern of this wonderful, generous lady.

Until her death two decades later, many of us wrote regularly to Miss Harrison, and several from our group visited her after the war.

BUZZ BOMBS

It had been a bad night. The German buzz bombs had hit all around London, quite a few close enough to shake our barracks. That morning, everyone came to work a bit bleary-eyed and subdued. Everyone, that is, but Tony, a corporal in the motor pool. He was scheduled for an early morning trip with one of the colonels, and when he was close to an hour late, his irate sergeant started looking for him.

"Nope, he isn't here," his barracks mates said. "He went into London to see his girl last night and didn't come back."

Semidiscreet inquiries revealed that the corporal, a happily married man from Tennessee, had been shacking up with an English girl quite regularly. And sure enough, one of the buzz bombs had landed on her apartment building the night before and killed them both in her bed.

The ticklish problem of whether or not to tell Tony's family the exact details of his death was discussed at headquarters for several days. Finally, it was decided to send the death notice to his wife telling her just that her husband had been killed by a German bomb while on leave in London.

Not long after we arrived in England, "the blitz" (the heavy bombing raids) began to diminish, and V-1 buzz bomb raids began. These German buzz bombs did much physical damage in London and the surrounding area, but the psychological damage to the inhabitants of that area was even more important.

You could hear the damn things ticking while they were still many miles away, and everybody would automatically start listening. Suddenly, the ticking would stop, and you started counting. Usually by the time you had counted to ten you would hear it detonate—hopefully a long way off. Now and again the bomb would glide longer than the usual ten seconds, or it would be a dud so no explosion would be heard. Then you just held your breath and prayed.

The bombs came any time day or night, but it was worse at night. If the bomb went on by, you could hear sighs all over our barracks, but if the ticking stopped, all twenty girls stopped breathing as they counted to ten. No matter how sound asleep you were, you would wake up when that awful ticking started. Nobody would say a word. Sometimes, if a number of bombs had gone over that night, someone would break into sobs. After the bomb finally exploded, some soft voice would say, "It's okay now. Thank God we're safe." There would be a community sigh and everyone would drift off to sleep until the next one.

These unmanned rocket bombs were terror weapons made in large numbers by the Germans near Peenemünde in Germany and launched toward England from northern coastal areas of Europe. The deep ticking sound of the buzz bombs, caused by their pulse-jet engines, could be heard for miles, the sound echoing frighteningly from buildings and down streets. In 1944, many thousands of V-1s were launched against Britain. Although they actually had little real military effect and caused only minor death and damage in London in comparison to the regular bomber raids of the blitz, German scientists could not have designed a better weapon to destroy morale and shatter nerves. It says a lot for English people's doggedness and determination that they endured this phase of the war so courageously. Maybe their courage came from the fact that they had lived through something much worse—the blitz, when the German Luftwaffe had rained incendiary bombs (thousands in each raid!) on London. These bombs had a magnesium core that burned at about 4,000 degrees F. Following these incendiary raids, the Germans had blanketed London with huge high-explosive bombs for a while. It's a wonder that London and Londoners lived and still fought on after all that.

The English people always tried hard to maintain their calm, but their uneasiness sometimes showed through. One typical afternoon, Helen, a pretty blonde girl from New Jersey, and I were at the Ritz, a posh London hotel. Very proper English ladies and gentlemen were enjoying a spot of tea at the tables around us. A polite buzz of conversation filled the air. As I started to sip my tea, we all became aware of the ticking of a buzz bomb coming closer and closer. My hand holding the teacup stopped halfway to my mouth. I noticed the gentleman at the next table, about to enjoy a bite of cake—with his fork motionless in midair, and the waiter standing as if frozen at the door to the kitchen with a tray full of cups (not one of which rattled). There was absolute silence for ten seconds. Then we heard the bomb detonate a short distance away. The gentleman put the forkful of cake into his mouth. I sipped my tea. The waiter started serving a nearby table. Conversations continued on from midsentence, as though they had never been broken off. Everything continued as though those seconds had never occurred.

Bushey, Herts, was just far enough northwest of London that we never did get a direct bomb hit, but there were a number of near misses. We could watch raids on London and could even see some of the big barrage balloons, looking like blimps, tethered at various altitudes over the heart of the city to discourage low-flying planes.

The last of the big blitz bombing runs by German planes were still going over the London area when we first arrived. A few of these German bombing runs went as far as northern Scotland, but most of them were concentrated in the London area. We watched many bombing raids over the city, but the German planes usually turned around over our area to head for home without dropping any bombs near us—because they had already dumped their whole load on poor London. Later, V-1 buzz bombs took their place. Then, in September 1944, V-2s (silent ballistic rockets) began. With sophisticated, liquid-fired rocket engines made in slave labor factories in the Hartz Mountains of Germany, V-2s had more explosive power and could be targeted more accurately, but somehow they were not so frightening as the V-1 buzz bombs.

Because of erratic weather, the big blitz bombing raids did not come every night, but some nights there would be two or three. When a raid was about to begin, the sirens would start to wail. The ululating sound began far off in South London, then came closer and closer, and got louder and louder. At night, huge spotlights would be turned on, and all over the black sky beams of light would dance, frantically trying to pinpoint the planes so the big guns on the ground could get them in their sights. When one light spotted a plane, a score of other lights would zero in immediately. Big antiaircraft guns would start to boom, and on the ground red and yellow bombs would start bursting and detonating. British Spitfires and Hurricanes would dart all over the sky like small birds harassing marauding crows. They were always outnumbered, but they were so fast and so determined that they always inflicted much more damage than they received.

The air would be filled with flak and tracer bullets and now and then a burst of flame—a plane blowing apart. Then the raid would end and the German planes would take off for home and safety. It was a beautiful sight, like a Fourth of July fireworks display—if you could ignore the horror behind the scenery.

Sometimes a raid would go on for hours with wave after wave of bombers. What a relief when things finally started slowing down and we knew another air raid was over and we were still alive! As soon as the steady all-clear sirens sounded, everyone would start assessing losses and damages. I don't know how the people of London could stand it night after night after night for months and years. Sirens day and night. All-night raids. Frightful explosions. Roped-off streets. Acres of burning buildings. Long civilian death lists. Whole blocks of nothing but smoking rubble, broken windows everywhere, shutters, taped-up windows, blackout curtains. But people made a point of "carrying on as usual."

A few times I got caught in air raids in London. At the sound of the sirens, most people automatically headed for air raid shelters (which were everywhere) or for subways. Others fatalistically stayed where they were, turned off the lights or put up heavy blackout curtains, and waited it out.

London's fire brigades were really efficient. After a hit, they were always right there to check for casualties, to look for and report unexploded bombs, to fight the fires, then to clear away as much of the rubble as they could to keep traffic moving. In parts of London, it seemed like half the buildings were either boarded up or gone—merely craters. During one of the worst raids of the blitz, St. Paul's Cathedral was set afire. Workers with sacks of sand saved it, with help from local volunteers who kicked the incendiary bombs off the steep roof.

Many thousands of Londoners worked during the day and slept in underground stations each night. These stations were eerie. People trying to catch trains in the subway tunnels crowded along the edges of the platforms next to the tracks, while platform areas next to the walls were crowded with sleeping people wound up in their blankets with their heads next to the walls. Many whole families were there with a little food and a few of their most prized possessions. Some people even had small canned heat burners to heat water for tea. There were very few cases of robbery or fighting in those stations. Early in the evening there might be some light chatter, but late at night all you could hear were snores, a baby crying somewhere, and the sounds of the air raid going on overhead. The subway management cooperated by dimming the lights so people could sleep. You would find it hard to imagine a gloomier, more in-hospitable place, but many Londoners slept there every night for years. After the roar of a train passing through, it was silent, gloomy, cold, damp, shadowy, and depressing.

In spite of the raids, most Londoners remained cheerful and optimistic. The fight for survival didn't allow them time to be bothered with self-pity, nor could they waste energy or time being unpleasant. They did what they could to help each other through this crisis, knowing that other persons' losses and tragedies were just as great as their own. I will always have the greatest admiration for their cheerful spirit and dogged deter-mination. They were amazing!

Wartime England was frightening, exciting, inspiring, edu-cational, surprising, but never dull.

MAJOR B

The first month after arriving in England, I worked in the of-fice of "Major B" while I awaited security clearance for cryp-tography. It was a routine office job and not very interesting. Major B, an army bureaucrat in his early forties, did not seem to be overly busy, so I was able to handle most of the work, with occasional help from another WAC.

At first, Major B treated me in a very businesslike manner. I knew the job was temporary, and I did not particularly like the man, so the cold, strictly business attitude of the office suited me just fine.

About the third week, Major B started getting more friendly. His wife in Boston sent him a steady supply of delicious foods, and he began sharing them with me. Soon he started offering me other things she had sent, like women's silk stockings, nice handkerchiefs, toiletries, etc. It offended me to think he would want to give away these gifts his wife had so lovingly sent him, so I refused as politely as possible. (I wondered what he had told her to get her to send some of these articles.)

Before long he was insinuating that he could arrange an advancement for a friend. A few days later he openly promised to make me a warrant officer if I would "be nice to him."

Within a few days he was chasing me around the office and pawing at me when I was not alert enough to avoid him, and inviting me out on dates or weekends, which I always refused as politely as possible. The more he pushed, the less I wanted to have anything to do with him. I despised the man.

It is hard to maintain one's dignity and proper military courtesy while dodging around a desk. I didn't know what to do besides using fast footwork. In the army, a corporal's word didn't amount to much against a major's word, and the whole thing embarrassed me. I talked to some of my friends about the situation and was considering going to Sergeant Reddy for advice when orders came for me to move on to cryptography. What a relief!

So I could have become a warrant officer—but I was happy to end the war as a corporal instead. Major B was sent back to Boston the next spring and given a disability discharge. I heard he died of a heart attack later that year. I didn't mourn the old goat.

CRYPTO

Everyone at the Eighth Air Force headquarters at Bushey worked hard. It was obvious a tremendous amount needed to be done in preparation for D-day and the campaigns to follow. Time was limited, and nobody could be comfortable not doing his or her best.

After receiving my security classification, I was assigned to the cryptographic section. Six cryptographic technicians (code clerks), two WACs and four GIs, worked in two tiny secret rooms in the basement of the castle. Specially reinforced concrete walls at least three feet thick surrounded us on top, bottom, and all four sides, with no outside windows or vents. To enter, we had to pass through three guarded doors, then knock on the code room door and be identified by voice before we were allowed to come in. The door was always locked immediately after we entered.

We worked around the clock in shifts, with two people always there to receive and send secret messages. Communications came in or went out in various codes, some on teletype machines, some written or typed. We decoded or encoded them and sent them on to the proper persons. In those hectic days just before D-day, we could barely keep up with the huge volume of classified messages coming in and going out at all hours of the day and night. Many of the codes were in long series of five-letter groups: MCMOD RFVLO CDRMA, and so on. Accuracy was essential. One letter wrong, and the meaning of the whole message could be lost. Sometimes it took considerable time and effort to discover which code was being used, especially if the signal had become garbled in any way during transmission. It was work that took a great deal of patience and concentration, and it was tiring.

Now, when I try to remember some of those messages, my mind is a complete blank. I translated and routed messages by the thousands, but I don't remember any of them. The code-room personnel were so thoroughly indoctrinated with the absolute necessity of never talking about any message we handled that we never, ever thought about them or mentioned them outside of that small room. What we read in that room, stayed in that room.

I vaguely remember that the subjects of those messages included troop movements and logistics, weather forecasts, and petrol reserves. The code room was often a madhouse when messages started coming in all at once. We had to watch that the messages made sense, were not garbled, and were sent on to the right person. Sometimes it was difficult to find the right code to use. If a message was unidentified, we sent it on up with no questions asked, no speculations, and no discussion.

When messages came in bunches, sometimes we could not keep up. But sometimes there were several hours when nothing arrived. During these slow periods, time dragged by very slowly indeed in that tiny enclosed room. We would play cards or write letters or talk. One of the soldiers I often worked with was nicknamed "Moose" for obvious reasons: He was an ex-football star. The constriction of that tiny code room really got to Moose, and he would pace the floor in frustration. That requires a lot of turns and short steps—three steps this way, three steps that way—in a ten foot by ten foot room. When he got tired of pacing, Moose would play his game of catching the flies that somehow found their way into that box. He would try to outdo his own record as an ace (five kills in a row) as he caught them in his hands, tossed them in the garbage, and announced his score on the way to an oak-leaf cluster for the day.

Because of the heavy concrete around us, we could just barely hear the buzz bombs coming in or the air raid sirens. But the bombs were an everyday fact of life, and our ears were attuned to their sound, so we never missed hearing them. When one hit nearby, the old building would rattle and cement dust and small pieces of concrete would sift down on us. It was a scary feeling to think about all those thick walls and locked doors between us and the outside if a bomb ever hit the building. If a buzz bomb got *too* close, we would both dive for the small space underneath the table we used as a desk. Moose and I butted heads many times as we landed in that tiny space. He'd say, "Do you realize how many tons of concrete are between us and the outside?" And I'd reply, "Forget it, Moose. Let's get on with the fly count." Since neither Moose nor I was really small, when we dived under the same little table there was always some hangout, so we usually got the giggles . . . after things settled a bit.

English fogs can be really *thick*: We quickly understood why the Brits called them "pea soupers." Many nights as we walked down familiar Bushey streets, we were able to find our way home only by walking with one foot in the gutter and the other on the curb. Even directly underneath the street lights, only a small, faint glow was visible. If you held your hand in front of your face a foot from your nose, you literally could not see it.

One night, after working the evening shift in the code room until midnight, I started to walk back to the barracks. As I opened the outside castle door, I found an English fog so thick that it was hard to breathe. It was a night to walk home by radar. I started off across the castle courtyard toward the exit in the opposite corner. This courtyard was about thirty feet by thirty feet, with crosswalks, trees, and bushes. I had crossed this space hundreds of times, but that night something turned me around. Maybe I was tired, or maybe one foot slipped off the edge of the walk. Whatever it was, suddenly I became totally disoriented.

No problem, I thought. *I'll just feel around for a wall or the trees or the bushes and get reoriented.* So I found a wall and started following it, but for some reason I couldn't find a door or the narrow entryway. Maybe bushes diverted me. I must have stumbled around that small space for over half an hour, totally frightened and lost for the first and only time in my life, stumbling into bushes, banging into trees where trees shouldn't have been. I was close to total panic, when suddenly off in the distance I heard the faint whistle of a train at the Bushey underground station about a mile away. The next second I knew exactly where I was. I just turned and walked directly out of that frightening square and back to the barracks. By counting posts and crosswalks, I had no more problems.

CODES AND CIPHERS

One day, after several months in the code section at Bushey, Mary Medora Stuart (the other WAC in the code room) and I were ordered to report to the officer in charge of cryptography for our headquarters.

"Corporals Stuart and Porter," he began, "I have selected you to represent this HQ at the upcoming British Codes and Ciphers School at Oxford. You will receive training in the basic

British codes. You will be ready by 0800 tomorrow morning for one month's TDY [temporary duty] at Oxford."

"Yes, sir!" we gulped in unison.

"You will be billeted with an older Englishwoman named Mrs. Medford. You will receive English food ration cards for the period you will be there. Give them to Mrs. Medford upon arrival. A British army driver will pick you up each morning at 0745 and take you back to your quarters at 1830."

"Now," he continued, "I want you to understand that up to this time, no WACs, and very few other Americans from any other service, have been allowed to attend this school. You understand that what you learn there will be secret information to be handled as such. As your commanding officer, I expect you both to behave in such a manner as to be a credit to the United States Army Air Force. Upon arrival at Oxford your driver will take you to the British HQ where you will report to the British liaison officer on duty before checking into your billet. Here are your orders. Good luck, corporals. Dismissed."

As soon as we were out of his office, Mary and I looked at each other in astonishment. "I can't believe what I just heard," she gasped. "Tomorrow morning! We're going to *Oxford!*"

"Wow!" I choked out.

We didn't sleep much that night because of our excitement, but at 0800 we were waiting at our company office for the army jeep to pick us up, all our buttons and insignia and shoes polished to gleaming perfection, our hats at exactly the proper angle.

The British Codes and Ciphers School at Oxford was an interservice training school. Representatives from all the British armed services, as well as Canadian and Australian personnel and half a dozen Americans from various services, were there, about seventy-five students altogether. Only the best from the various code groups represented had been chosen for this school, and it was considered an honor to be included. Classes required a great deal of concentration. This was no kiddie's course, but intensive, no-nonsense training. Competition was tough. Everyone was well aware of how important to the war effort this knowledge was, and each student was doing his or her very best.

Classes ran from 0800 to 1730, with a short break for morning and afternoon teas and a half hour for lunch. By the time we arrived at our billet each evening we were exhausted. No time for social life, just to bed as early as possible so we could keep up with everything the next day.

Colonel Wellingham, a British army officer commissioned during the Boer War, had volunteered to return to service from retirement to help out during the emergency. He kept a tight rein on things. No nonsense allowed. Still, he was well liked and respected.

Classes were even held Saturday mornings, but immediately after lunch on that day, all members of the school stood for review on the parade grounds. It was spring, so some Saturdays were warm in the early afternoon. When British troops stand at attention they are rigid, not nearly as relaxed as American soldiers on review. After a few minutes, some of the British troops would start to waver, and if we stood there too long they would start to drop—not just collapsing, but crashing down flat on their faces, still "at attention." The two soldiers on either side of the fallen one would quietly pick him up and take him to the rear to be revived.

Colonel Wellingham had become quite obese in retirement. Close to three hundred pounds and well over retirement age, he did not find it easy to review the troops, although he enjoyed it. To match his gait, the colonel's favorite song, "Moonlight and Roses," was played slowly and rhythmically by the small British army post band as part of each Saturday's review. The colonel would slowly roll along to the music, still managing to look proper and dignified. The first Saturday we stood for review, Mary and I had a hard time keeping straight faces when he came rolling by. We did not dare smile or break formation, although I thought I saw a twinkle in his eyes as he passed.

Our landlady, Mrs. Medford, a sweet elderly Englishwoman, tried very hard to make us feel at home. She provided us with breakfast and dinner, which, despite the severe rationing, were adequate and well prepared.

I always felt guilty at Mrs. Medford's. The first evening we were there, she started to pour our cups of tea. "And how do you like your tea, dearie?" she asked. Later I realized she meant "How many lumps of sugar would you like?"

"Just plain. No milk or sugar," I replied.

Well! All her life the dear old lady had served tea with the teapot in her right hand and a pitcher of warm milk in the other hand, pouring them into the cup at the same time to mix them properly. This strange desire of mine for no milk completely befuddled her.

"Oh, my! I've poured your tea with milk after all. Here, I'll pour another cup." Sometimes it took three or four cups before she could restrain that left hand with the milk pitcher, but she would always persist until she got it right. To my embarrassment, this happened every night we were in Oxford. I kept hoping she would forget about my odd notion, but she always remembered and tried to do it just right.

The only free time we had while in Oxford was on Sundays. Mary and I usually spent that day wandering around the colleges and town of Oxford, fascinated by the history and beauty of the place. The ancient halls, magnificent walkways and arches, the general air of solemn antiquity were awe-inspiring. We felt that we ought to speak in whispers in such a respected place of wisdom. Oxford has thirty-five independent colleges, but because of the war most of them had very few students. The libraries and halls were still open, and a few scholars still wandered around the campus, strolling along, ignoring the world as they thought their deep thoughts. Now and then we enjoyed conversations with shopkeepers or other local people who were intrigued by these American women living in their midst, but most of these days were spent just absorbing the aura of the place.

One Sunday we chanced to go down to the banks of the Thames, where a boat race was being held between the Oxford sculling crew and several other school crews. It was fascinating to watch the precision of these rowing crews, and we got very excited as we watched the boats surging ahead of each other.

We started to yell, "Yeah, Number Six! Come on! You can win! Come on!"

But then we noticed the other onlookers. The proper English ladies in their hats and furs and gloves clapped gently at exciting moments, murmuring, "Well done, Number Five." And the British gentlemen, in well-modulated voices, would say, "I say, old chaps! Good show!"

After a few lusty "Come on, Number Six's" and some astonished but polite stares, we tried to restrain our enthusiasm.

The last evening of the school we were invited to a graduation party at a small nearby clubhouse. The little British army post band played and there were sandwiches, ale, cakes, and other refreshments. All the students, as well Colonel Wellingham, the school officers, and other personnel, were there, having a good time. Everyone relaxed after the strains of the past few weeks and all enjoyed a few hours of forgetting the war and just having fun. Not a wild party by American standards, just a "nice," happy evening before we all went our various ways.

Toward the end of the evening, the colonel suddenly appeared before me. "May I have the honor of this dance, ma'am?" he inquired, then turned to the band and ordered, "Come on, boys. Play my favorite song. Play 'Boompsie Dazie'!"

What an experience! "Boompsie Dazie" was a dance popular in England at that time. "Hands, knees, and *boompsie* dazie," you sang as you clapped hands with your partner, slapped your knees, then turned quickly and butted rears. The colonel was having a wonderful time . . . all three hundred pounds of him. Every time we "boomped" I'd go flying across the dance floor, trying desperately to stay on my feet and not knock someone over. Then back to the colonel for another chorus! He roared with laughter, and I couldn't help but laugh with him. As a matter of fact, everyone in the room laughed as hard as we did. Each time I was sent zooming across the floor, they would clear a path for me, anticipating the targeting. At the end of the song, the colonel was purple and out of breath from laughing, and so was I. "Thank you, little lass," he said. "Seems as though you're a bit unsteady on your feet." And he waddled off, roaring with laughter at his own joke.

It was rather a letdown to return to the routine at Bushey the next day. No more being waited on by Mrs. Medford. No milky tea. No morning and afternoon tea breaks. But it was good to see our friends. From then on, Mary and I handled all British messages in the code room.

The only other time I saw Oxford was from a plane one Sunday afternoon later that summer.

My friend Mary Ann had been dating a U.S. Army Air Force pilot from a nearby air base. Bill called her early that Sunday morning and asked if she would like to go flying that afternoon. She was thrilled at the idea. He said he would pick her up at noon, "and by the way, my friend Chuck will be along, too, so bring a friend. We can get a plane for a couple of hours, and it's a great day for flying."

After several weeks of steady rain and fog, the sun had finally come out of hiding, and it was an unbelievably beautiful day. Bill and Mary Ann rode in the back seat of the single-engine Norseman plane. Chuck piloted the plane, and I rode in the copilot's seat. We flew aimlessly around the English Midlands for a while, enjoying the scenery and the great day. Of course we were careful to stay well away from London. We didn't want to be mistaken for a German plane.

Soon, however, the gorgeous day, the fun and freedom of joyriding around in a plane, and just pure high spirits got a little out of hand.

We were flying low over some meadows when Chuck spied a small herd of cows grazing peacefully on a low hill. The temptation was too much! He buzzed them. Have you ever seen a herd of cows running pell-mell in all directions with their tails straight up in the air like a bunch of flagpoles? It was a ridiculous sight, and we laughed so hard we cried.

Then Chuck really got carried away. We were flying over the Thames near Oxford, where a number of English people were enjoying the lovely day punting on the river. Men in bowlers slowly rowed along the peaceful river with their lady friends who were replete with hats and parasols.

Down we roared! The ladies jumped out of the boats on one side, and the gentlemen jumped out on the other side, evidently convinced that the plane was going to land right on top of them. It was like a scene from an old Keystone Cops movie.

Suddenly a bridge loomed just ahead. It was a single-span stone bridge with a low arch over the river. "Hey, hot shot. You'll never make it!" yelled Bill from the back seat.

"Sure I will, pal!" Chuck yelled back. "I'm the best damned pilot in the air force."

And under the bridge we zoomed. I am sure there was no more than a foot of space between each wingtip and the bridge supports. And not much more space above and below us.

"You sure *must* be the best pilot in the air force to get through there," I gasped after I caught my breath. "But let's not try it again soon, okay?"

"Told ya I could make it," Chuck grinned. "Oh, hell, boys and girls. It's been fun, but we're getting low on fuel, so we gotta go home now."

"Just don't tell anyone about our ride, okay, girls?" Bill said after we landed. "It was sort of 'unofficial.'"

Mary Ann and I agreed we had never seen anything as funny as those cows, and we both felt guilty about the boaters, even though that was funny too—from our perspective. But the bridge was unbelievable! *Never want to try that again*, we decided. *Once was more than enough.*

PEEKS AT SCOTLAND AND WALES

What do I really know about Wales, I asked myself.

Well, my grandmother used to tell me about *her* Welsh grandmother reading from an old Welsh Bible. "The book was at least two feet tall," my grandmother said, "and each page was only about eight inches wide. Sometimes one word would be long enough to cover a whole page."

I knew little else about the country except that it covered a peninsula on the southwestern edge of England, and that some famous poets had come from there.

Helen had three days' leave time coming. I could manage the same time off, so she suggested that we extend our sightseeing and explore a little of Wales. Our timing of the trip was poor because the weather was cold and gloomy and wet.

We spent most of our time in and around Cardiff, a coal-mining town nestled between low mountains and the seacoast on the southern edge of Wales. We wandered through the streets and shops, took short bus trips in the near vicinity, explored some grim old castles, and browsed through several museums, but we did not enjoy our time there. Part of our problem was the awful weather, and part was the generally run-down, unimpressive, coal-dust-covered buildings and the dourness of the people. Even the ships down at the docks seemed small, dingy, poor, uninteresting. It was a disappointing trip.

In contrast, Mary Stuart and I spent a week in Scotland that was even better than we had hoped. Mary had a number of Scottish ancestors, and I had a few of my own from that part of the world, so we were anxious to go there and see the places and things we had heard about all our lives.

The train from London to Edinburgh amazed us. It was fast, it was smooth, it was on time, it was comfortable—and it had movie screens at the front of each car, which even American planes did not have at that time, so we were duly impressed.

In Edinburgh (we learned that the "burgh" was pronounced "burrow") we had a B&B (bed and breakfast) room in a private home near the center of town. Most commercial accommodations were filled with priority military personnel, so we were lucky to find this home. Our room had two double beds with lots of wool blankets and huge pillows, a bowl and basin on the bath stand, and fresh flowers every day. What heat there was came from a small fireplace. In the evening only enough fire was built to barely take the chill off the space nearest the fire, so there was no dawdling about getting ready for bed and popping under the warm covers where a bedwarmer brick had heated up a little space at the foot.

Our landlady quietly "knocked us up" (waked us up, that is) each morning at seven to inquire if we were ready for our tea. She served us steaming hot cups of tea in bed, then quickly started the fire in the fireplace to take a little chill off the room. As we sipped our tea, she went downstairs and returned a few minutes later with a trayful of newly baked, hot buttered scones with jam. After barracks life, this was sheer luxury. By the time we consumed this delicious breakfast, we were ready to face any adventures the day could provide.

Exploring Edinburgh itself was an adventure. The city is on the Firth of Forth, a bay surrounded by beautiful countryside. Edinburgh Castle, high on Castle Rock overlooking the city, had an aura of antiquity. Part of its fascinating history was that Mary, Queen of Scots, had also enjoyed the magnificent views from its towers. We walked the Royal Mile leading from the castle to the center of town, and on to Holyrood Palace. As we walked along, Mary murmured dreamily, "We should be wearing snoods and long flowing dresses so we'll be ready to meet that knight in shining armor who must be waiting at the next corner." The ancient buildings, streets, and castles of this city made us feel as though medieval times might still exist in this lovely old place. As we meandered along, enjoying the shops, awed by the churches and monuments, we talked to the friendly, outgoing Scots men and women along the way. Now and then we joined them for tea or a bit of ale at a local pub.

Another day we traveled to central Scotland to visit an ancient castle near Stirling that had everything a castle *should* have: a moat, secret rooms, towers, a drawbridge, a dungeon—everything! Secret passageways led through the base of the walls to provide an avenue of escape to the small village at the foot of the high hill on which the castle stood (in case enemies were about to overrun the walls during a siege). In a side court-yard, a two-foot-square hole covered with rusty grating was the only entrance or exit to the twelve-foot-square dungeon in the rocks about thirty feet below. Prisoners were fed by dropping food through the grating. The only way out was to have a long rope lowered from the surface. We were informed that this escape rope had been used but rarely. As we peered into the gloomy depths of the dungeon, we could almost imagine that we could see ancient skeletons in the shadows, or hear faint groans of anguish. If anyone had yelled "boo!" we would have had heart attacks.

The ladies of the court had spent most of their time in a high tower room. With cold gray rock walls and no glass window-panes, it was breezy up there. When the castle was used as a home and a court, the walls and floors had been covered with tapestries and woolens, but that breeze must have made it a very cold, miserable place on winter days and nights.

The moat had been dry for years, but the drawbridge over it and the huge castle gates with their peepholes and chains were still intact. We even saw the old horse stables at one end of the courtyard with armaments for the horses and men who protected the place.

This castle visit was most satisfying. Everything we had ever heard or dreamed about castles came to life for us that day.

After the dream world of Edinburgh and its castles, Glasgow, on the River Clyde in western Scotland, seemed all bustle, noise, and excitement with a lively personality all its own.

Another day, we visited the Scottish Highlands and Loch Lomond. We took a boat trip down the lake and enjoyed breathtaking views of the rolling mountains. That afternoon was spent gathering furze and heather as we wandered around the hills near the foot of the lake. We even climbed a small nearby mountain. At tea time in a small shop, we heard tales of Highlanders and little people, sea monsters presumably dwelling in the lake, problems under English rule, and the hopes that Scotland someday would become more independent from its southern neighbor.

Our Scottish holiday ended much too soon. Long before we were ready, we found ourselves on the train back to London. A contingent of Scottish soldiers headed back to their units to prepare for D-day were our fellow passengers. All of these men had fought in other battles of the war in North Africa, Italy, and Dunkirk, and they understood where they would be going next. D-day was imminent. Two American WACs were a welcome diversion. They shared their snacks, their jokes and stories, and their songs with us as we sped southward. Our trouble with the Scottish accents greatly amused them when they tried to teach us to sing the drinking song "Aye belang to Glazga, dear ol Glazga doon, Wha's the matter wi' Glazga? It's go-en' roon n' roon."

"Maybe we helped cheer them up a bit," Mary said later.

"They're really nice boys. I hope we took their minds off the war for a little while," I agreed. After a moment of silence, we both sighed. We knew that we must head back to our own part of the work of preparing for D-day. We must return to the bombings again. Scotland had seemed so safe and so far away from the war, although it really wasn't. There had been air raids up there, too, and everyone in Scotland was involved in the war in one way or another.

Mary broke the silence with a half-hearted grin. "I'll never be able to sing 'Glazga' right without their help though. I just hope they'll all get home again."

"LET'S GO INTO LONDON."

London, with its sights, sounds, smells, history, amusements, and people from all over the world, was a magnet.

It was easy to get there from Bushey: Just walk down to the underground station a mile away and wait for one of the frequent trains. Part of the underground is above ground in the suburbs, and it was a pleasant forty-five-minute trip. That particular line received few bomb hits, although other stations and lines were often out of commission for a few days or weeks because of bombing. When this happened, people in that area used the old, green, double-decker buses with their steep stairs and distinctive horns.

One of the stations we went through on our way to central London was Wembley. A favorite joke was about two deaf old men traveling on the underground. One asks the other "Is this Wembley?" "No, it's Thursday." "So am I. Let's stop for a drink, shall we?"

No matter how often we went to London, the city never failed to provide us with excitement and fun and adventure— in spite of the war. Refugees, armed force members, diplomats, artists from all over the world filled the city. Just watching the crowds was fascinating. Sometimes we wandered up and down streets, finding buildings or places we had read about in books, or discovering odd little shops or tea rooms. Sometimes, we headed for the big Red Cross canteen on Piccadilly Circus where there was always a crowd of American servicepeople as well as coffee and doughnuts, dancing, and lists of the latest entertainments offered in the London area. Now and then free tickets were available to the theater or special events.

One invitation to an art exhibit helped Helen and me meet a couple of handsome French soldiers who had escaped from Paris to form a group of Frenchmen working with Allied forces in England. We spent an afternoon and evening with them wandering around London. We tried hard to communicate (their English, poor as it was, was far better than our French) and talked about our respective homes and families. They had to leave for their base early that evening, and we never saw them again. But we were greatly impressed by their glamour and sophistication, plus their dedication to freeing their country from German occupation.

Another small adventure in London was when a GI took me to a play one evening and then to one of the gentlemen's clubs in Pall Mall (pronounced "pell mell") for a drink. It was probably a club for gentlemen only, judging from the horrified looks on everyone's faces and the sudden silence when I came in, and since there were no other women present. However, the English gentlemen were far too polite to make a scene by throwing out two American allies, so a nervous bartender served us our drinks. And I persuaded my escort to leave as soon as possible to relieve the sticky situation.

One evening, Helen, Verna, and I were lucky enough to get tickets to a stage show as part of the group of six guests of the stars of the show. After the play we were invited backstage to meet the cast and to have tea with the stars. Heady stuff for a Montana ranch girl!

With so many stars of the European performing arts living there as refugees, wartime London was a great place for theater lovers. We had the opportunity to enjoy performances by the greatest ballet stars, symphony orchestras, dancers, singers, and actors of all Europe. However, we tried to plan theater trips when no air raids were expected. Several times bombs had fallen on English theaters, causing large numbers of casualties. In spite of this, we frequented the Savoy, Strand, Sadler Wells, and other famous London theaters. There was even one small movie house in London that was showing *Gone with the Wind*. It ran the same movie three times a day for the next twenty years. We also enjoyed a local little-theater group in Bushey that produced a new play each week. We became so familiar with this small group of actors, as well as with most of the local audience, that we felt like part of the family.

For art lovers, wartime London was rather disappointing. Most works of art that could be moved had been taken to safer places or stored in underground vaults. Those that could not be moved, such as the statue of Eros in Piccadilly Circus, were covered with wooden frameworks to help keep them as safe as possible.

Even in wartime, London was a sightseer's delight. We spent many long days admiring Westminster Cathedral, London Bridge, the City of London, and a myriad of spots in between, absorbing the flavor of life in Soho, Piccadilly, and other sections of town, each with its own distinct personality.

St. Paul's Cathedral, the Tower of London, Royal Albert Hall, the Houses of Parliament, Nelson's Column, the River Thames all fascinated us, as did the famous changing of the guards at the Royal Palace.

Many museums were still open, even though their most precious exhibits were gone, but Mme Tussaud's Wax Museum was still in full swing. We often spent long hours wandering through London parks and gardens. Mary and I even went to the zoo one day, but were shocked to find that most of the animals had been removed to safer spots or slaughtered. There was not enough food for the animals, and the Londoners needed meat, so the least rare animals had to be sacrificed.

Of course, the English pubs helped everyone's morale. The equivalent of American clubhouses, community centers, and neighborhood bars all rolled into one, they were warm, friendly, happy places in which to spend a few hours, sing a few songs, and discuss life and the problems of staying alive.

Bitters (dry ale) was usually not enjoyed by the Yanks, nor was dark, heavy-bodied stout or porter (a weaker stout). Lager was lighter, more like the beer at home. English ale was good, too, but stronger and heavier than American beer. Scotch and Irish whiskeys were readily available, as was rum, although the wartime rum was terrible, rank, and bitter. "'Arf 'n 'arf" was a bit of a shock to American beer drinkers at first, but we soon got used to the lukewarm stuff. And we passed the word around in a hurry about which bartenders collected the drippings under the counter and added leftover spirits from drinking glasses— to serve to unwary customers toward the end of the evening. Our efforts at playing the ancient pub game of darts were usually met with polite amusement by Brits who had grown up with the game, but we enjoyed trying to hit the target anyway.

One day, Verna and I chanced to be at the Piccadilly Circus Canteen when an invitation came in for half a dozen service people to observe an English court case. This was of particular interest to Verna since she was a court reporter, so we jumped at the chance. Verna enjoyed the court proceedings, but I was so fascinated by all the "Oyez'es" and the ratty old curly white wigs the judge and barristers (lawyers) wore that I didn't pay much attention to the actual case. To me, the whole thing seemed just like a movie scene of an English court—too "English" and Dickensian to be real.

We spent another day near London touring a castle with an ancient boxwood maze. It was the first maze I had ever seen, and it fascinated me. We couldn't hear outside sounds as we sat on the old stone bench at the center of the maze; the high, thick hedges cut off sound and sights, and we were in a world apart. It was easy to believe the tales of lovers disappearing forever into the narrow aisles of the maze, or the legends of murders in long-ago times committed somewhere in the midst of the dark and gloomy walls of boxwood.

The Royal Botanical Gardens at Kew, just outside London, were fantastic even in wartime. These gardens truly deserve their status as among the finest in the world. The damp climate, as well as many years of careful planning and grooming, have created a place of impressive beauty. When we were there, the azaleas were in full bloom, and it was unbelievably lovely as we wandered down the paths for hours, entranced with all the colors and shapes and smells.

Few other people were about, so we were able to talk with some of the old gardeners working there. They were all past retirement age or partially disabled, since the younger gardeners had gone to the army, but as they talked about the trees, plants, and bushes and told us where the seeds or cuttings had come from and how they were transplanted and kept healthy, it was obvious that they loved this garden. Their pride in it was very apparent, even as they apologized for things not being in "the proper shape like 'twas before so many of the staff 'ad to go off ta fight the Germans."

"It's hard to see how it could be much more beautiful than it is. You're doing a great job and we love your garden!" we said, as they glowed in our admiration.

"EVERY LITTLE MOMENT HAS A MEANING ALL ITS OWN"

Sunny, warm days are not common in England, but when we were blessed with such a day, we appreciated it all the more. My friend Helen and I decided to spend one such glorious spring day in Kensington Gardens in central London just lying in the sun, basking in the warmth, wandering dreamily through the springtime lushness of the park and feeding the swans and ducks bits of the picnic we had brought along.

This day became the most perfect day of our stay in England.

Soon after we entered the park with all its flowers, trees, and bushes, we stopped on the edge of a small pond to admire the swans sailing serenely round and round.

Suddenly a laughing voice behind us said, "Well, *now* what do you Yanks think of our English weather?"

Turning, we saw an attractive young couple grinning at us. She was in a British Home Guards uniform, and he wore the uniform of an Aussie infantry officer.

"Nothing could be nicer than this day," Helen answered positively, smiling back at them.

"Come feed these bloody swans with us," the young man said, and before we knew it, we were throwing pieces of crackers into the water and laughing together at the ugly voices of the swans, so incongruous in those lovely bodies.

Soon we knew that Mavis was English and Eric was her Australian cousin, and that this was the first time they had seen each other since their early teens. They seemed to be so happy together and so fond of each other that Helen and I made excuses to leave them alone to enjoy their reunion, but they insisted on our joining them for a picnic. We added our bit to theirs, and they spread a cloth on the grass at the edge of the lake. The next few hours we ate, all talking at once or laughing about nothing or everything.

It was as if we had been close friends for years, sharing many of the same opinions, liking or disliking many of the same things, feeling free to argue loudly on some subjects—arguments that always ended with a laugh. A more congenial group could seldom be found.

After finishing off our picnic lunch and feeding the last few crumbs to the birds, we decided to take a walk. Arm in arm, four abreast, all in step, we sailed through the park and along the Serpentine, greeting civilians and armed forces personnel with broad smiles and happy hellos.

Most of the time we sang as we walked—any song we thought the others might know or that was popular. Eric and Mavis taught Helen and I their favorite song: "Every Little Moment Has a Meaning All Its Own." Its lilting tune was perfect for strolling. We even added a few extra fancy dance steps now and then just to fit our exuberant spirits, and to celebrate our friendship and the happiness of the day.

It was a gem of a day! I shall never forget it. Whenever I hear their song, I feel an irrepressible smiley feeling begin to spread all over me, and I feel young and aglow and happy with the wonderful world around me—in spite of troubles and wars and sadness. I remember sunshine and friendship and laughter—and the oneness of people from all over the world. And I am glad to be alive.

But even wonderful days have to end. When the lamplighters started their evening rounds, Mavis and Eric had to rush off. Eric was to sail for the Continent with his company early the next morning. Mavis had to report to her Guards company. And Helen and I had to return to Bushey, Herts, for bed check.

We parted most reluctantly, and the special glow of that day stayed with us for weeks.

A few months later Helen and I ran into Mavis on a trip to London. The lightness had gone from her smile, and her eyes had a shadow.

"Have you heard from Eric lately?" we asked.

Looking away, she replied, "Eric was killed in the fighting in France a week after our day in the park."

D-DAY

During the last months I was in England, tensions mounted noticeably. The code room found itself swamped with work. Each morning that the weather was halfway decent we could see and hear waves of planes passing overhead on their way to bomb Germany. Each afternoon we saw them coming back to their bases, their formations not nearly so neat and complete as on the way out. Sometimes it was obvious that a plane had been badly shot up. As we heard the engines sputtering or saw the plane wavering, we would wonder if they could make it back to their home field. Many of them didn't, but at least the ones we saw landed in friendly territory.

American, British, Canadian, Australian, and all the other Allied forces were busy day and night, knowing how important the upcoming invasion would be to the future of the whole world. Tensions, hopes, fears, worries kept mounting. Only a small number of leaders knew where or when D-day would occur, so the rest of us discussed the various possibilities and made wild guesses about what might happen.

Great Britain was crowded with several million armed men. Dozens of divisions were barracked in the United Kingdom. Thousands of vessels (most of them assault craft) awaited the coming invasion, as well as battleships, cruisers, and many destroyers. In the air, the allies had gathered thousands of fighters and bombers. Allied planes were busy pummeling the shores and heart of Europe.

Then D-day finally did come—June 6, 1944. We awakened early that morning to the steady, heavy droning of planes overhead. Hundreds and hundreds of planes flew low, heavily loaded with bombs, in perfect V-formations that seemed to fill the whole sky. For long hours, wave after wave after wave flew over us.

"I never knew there were so many planes in the whole wide world," Mary said softly.

"I'm sure glad I'm not on the Continent today," Verna replied in an awed voice.

"Well, this is the day we've all been hoping for and waiting for, and worrying about," added Helen. "May God be with those guys up there."

A low "Amen" echoed around the barracks. We knew what they were facing that day.

On D-day, the weather was awful—the seas high and wild and black, the winds strong and biting cold, but about 100,000 troops went ashore in northern France, with millions to follow. A twelve-hour aerial bombardment before they landed dropped thousands of tons of bombs. Our losses were great, but so were the German losses.

Then came grim months filled with news of horrible battles,

long lists of casualties, pictures in the papers of death and de-struction. Our forces were pushing the Germans out of north-ern France. Then—No! The Germans seemed to be winning the war. We were losing far too many lives and too much equip-ment. The Germans were breaking through our lines in Bel-gium. More and more casualties. Continual bombings on both sides of the Channel. Supplies couldn't seem to get where they were most needed fast enough.

Chaos. Fear. Destruction. Death.

All we could do was work as hard as possible and try to ap-pear cheerful. We had great faith in our country and its ability to eventually win this awful war. We *had* to win to save the world from that monster Hitler and his gang! The alternative was too gruesome to even think about. So we "carried on."

Many of the young men I knew and dated in England dis-appeared in the fighting in France. Like Delbert, a corporal in an infantry division. Delbert was a tall, gangly, thoroughly nice boy from Tennessee who developed a real crush on me at a company party near London before D-day. I liked him, but he wasn't someone I could get serious about. We went on several dates to movies or dances, and he kept proposing each time I saw him.

"Delbert, I like you, but I don't love you, and I don't want to marry you."

"Well, just be friends, then," he would say with a sigh.

His unit was one of the first to go ashore on D-day, and they were in the midst of the fighting until Germany surrendered. Delbert wrote to me whenever there was a lull. I answered his letters, but my answers were not as frequent as his letters, and I was never sure how often he received the letters I did write.

The last time I heard from Delbert, his letter arrived in a dirty envelope. A penciled note was scrawled on a tag-end of note paper. "I'm writing to you from a muddy foxhole, so please excuse this paper and pencil. Fighting has been bad. It's sure cold and wet here. We lost a lot of men already. I want you to remember I love you. Maybe after this war is over we'll be married and live happily ever after in the good ole U.S. of A. Don't forget me. I love you. Please write. Love, Delbert."

The same week that I got this letter, news came of terrible fighting in the Ardennes Forest in southeast Belgium during the battle of the Bulge. Thousands of our men were freezing in the frigid winter weather, and many lives were lost in the heavy fighting. According to news reports, that was where Delbert's unit was located.

I answered his letter, but I doubt that he ever received it. I never heard from him again. For years afterward, I felt guilty about not writing to him more often.

"SUFFICIENT UNTO THE DAY IS THE EVIL THEREOF"

Some things in this world are hard to explain. Like what happened one day in London where Helen and I were spending a free day.

We left Bushey early, and we spent most of the morning shopping and absorbing the sights, sounds, and smells of the city. After an hour in the famous Olde Curiosity Shoppe, we wandered on to other old pawn shops and secondhand stores loaded with wonderful treasures from all over the world. England was crowded with thousands of refugees from all over the continent of Europe. Many of these people existed only by selling family treasures one by one in the East End antique shops. Beautiful family heirlooms, jewelry, linens, silver, art treasures, all were available at very low prices. We bought a few things to send home, but could not afford nearly as many as we would have liked.

One GI in our HQ named Nathan had generous funding from home. He shipped box after box of these wonderful treasures back to the States. Shipping space to the United States was practically unlimited since ships were busy bringing war supplies to Europe and returned home only half loaded.

Nathan's enterprise bothered no one, and he must have made a fortune.

After lunch that day in a downtown hotel, Helen and I strolled down a side street to window shop. Around one corner we noticed a small sign:

MADAME LAROUX

—SECRETS OF YOUR PAST AND FUTURE—

—PALMISTRY—

—CARDS READ—

2ND FLOOR, RM. 14.

"That might be fun," Helen said. "Why don't we try it? We've got time before we have to catch the train back to Bushey."

"Ah, I don't believe in that stuff," I replied.

"Well, I don't either, but I've always been curious about fortune telling. It might be fun. Come on! Okay? I've never tried it before."

So up we went to Room 14. Madame LaRoux was a middle-aged, frowsy, tired-looking Englishwoman sitting at a small wooden table in a dank, shabby little room. A dingy cloth was thrown over the table, and as she talked she fondled a small crystal ball and a set of tarot cards.

"You will marry a handsome man and have two children," she told Helen. "You are generous and energetic . . ." She droned on, adding other generalities, the usual stuff to make girls our age giggle. It was about what we had expected: nothing spectacular or particularly interesting. Helen stood up, looking disappointed.

Now it was my turn. Madame L. read my fortune in the cards first. More banalities. Then she looked sharply at me as she said, "You will soon go on a short sea voyage." At that time I had no idea that any WACs would be sent to France anytime soon, and absolutely no inkling that I would be chosen to go, and not Helen.

Then Madame L. began to read my palm. At first her patter was just ordinary, uninspired statements about my supposed personality and abilities. Then, after a long pause, she said in a low voice, "You will have four children, and one more. You will be married once, and he will die young. You will have a serious illness in mid-life." I laughed, not taking her forecasts seriously.

Suddenly her face changed as she peered more closely at my palm. "Go now," she said abruptly. "I must not tell you more."

"But why not?" I asked. "Now you've got me really curious."

"No. No!" Obviously disturbed, she was anxious for me to leave. Then, rising slowly, she added softly, "I see much tragedy and darkness and pain. I must not tell you any more." She almost shoved us out the door as she mumbled, "I shouldn't have told you this much."

"Well! How about that?" Helen said, wide-eyed.

"Good thing I don't believe in that stuff or I'd be scared," I laughed.

I have never gone to another fortune teller. What she predicted has all come true.

Grace Virginia Porter, WAAC Auxiliary A-702462, during basic training
at Fort Des Moines, Iowa, the first WAAC training center, 1943

Verna Newman, Helen Fabaniek, and the author at the Eighth Air Force
Fighter Command, Bushey, Herts, Eng., 1943. Verna and Helen were court
reporters.

The author at Kew Gardens, 1944

The WAC members of the code room staff at Eighth Air Force HQ,
Bushey. Left to right: Corporal Mary Stuart, Lieutenant Mimi Gerber,
Lieutenant Mary Emerson, and Corporal Grace Porter.

Bomb damage at the Le Havre, France, waterfront, 1944

Photo by Donald Rule

Rear view of the house in Charleroi, Belgium, where the author's WAC detachment was billeted in 1945. Verna, Helen, and the author shared a small room on the fourth floor (marked with X). The bathroom was on the first floor.

Verna, Vera (last name not remembered), and the author on the Charleroi town square on Market Day

Ninth Air Force Headquarters building in Charleroi, 1945. The flag is at half-mast to mourn President Roosevelt's death.

Photo by Donald Rule

Ray, Don, and Casey at the armament plant they supervised in Charleroi. Casey and the author made a social foursome with Don and Verna, who married soon after the war. They celebrated their fiftieth wedding anniversary shortly before Verna died, a few years ago.

The author and Casey at Loverval Lake near Charleroi on one of the few nice days in the spring of 1945

Un pissoir—a common sight on streetcorners all over Belgium and France

Russian and Polish former POWs out for their daily walk in Charleroi. They included both men and women, and they usually sang lustily as they marched along. They were waiting for the eastern front to clear up so they could be sent home. This photo was taken across the street from the WAC billet.

The Charleroi town square on Victoire-Paix Day just after the parade. The crowds were even denser that evening, when a faulty fireworks display gave the author some frightening moments.

WACs stationed in Charleroi parade on Victoire-Paix Day. The author is in the middle of the front row.

3

WARTIME EUROPE

OFF TO BELGIUM

Dark gray clouds hovered less than a hundred feet above the wind-chopped waters of the English Channel. Here and there, fog banks rose to meet the clouds, and a wind blew icy spray across the wet decks of the LST (Landing Ship, Tank) as we tossed wildly in the turbulent seas.

It was early February 1945. England was still being bombed by the Germans. Our ship was part of a convoy that left a southern English port the afternoon before to zigzag its way across the channel toward Le Havre, which is at the mouth of the Seine River halfway between Dieppe and Cherbourg. The convoy carried troops and supplies to help counter the German breakthrough in the Ardennes, where fighting was heavy. The battle of the Bulge had begun in southeast Belgium in December. Paris had been liberated on August 25, 1944, but there were still many pockets of German resistance in France.

This first contingent of WAAF (Women's Army Air Force, formerly the WAC—the title was changed while I was in England) had been transferred from the Eighth Air Force in England to help the understaffed Ninth Air Force headquarters in Charleroi, Belgium. Twenty-four enlisted women, two

WAAF lieutenants, and one WAAF captain were chosen from various units in England for this group. I had been picked because I knew U.S. cryptography and had attended the British Codes and Ciphers School.

After a miserable day and night in our sardine-tin cabins, we came up to the aft deck of the LST for some air. Our cabin, not much bigger than a closet, had bunks five deep on each side, and one small, tightly sealed porthole. (Although designed to carry tanks, LSTs had been adapted to countless other uses, including troop transport.) When you lay on your side in your bunk, you bumped into the bottom of the person above. Our stuffed duffel bags completely filled the narrow aisle between the tiers of bunks. Helmets, canteens, mess gear, gas masks, and boots were stored on top of our feet on the narrow bunks. Thank God nobody got seasick.

Breakfast was the usual K rations. Then there was nothing to do but lie in our bunks staring at the wall or the bottom of the bunk above you. After a while our officers agreed to let us go up on deck for a little fresh air. We were warmly dressed in GI jackets, wool pants, "Lil' Abner" boots, wool caps, and helmets, and we were used to English winter weather. The crisp fresh air felt good after the stale smells of our cabins.

Now and then other ships in the convoy could be seen chopping through the waves a few miles fore and aft of us. As we watched the birds and fish in the water around us, we became aware of the sound of distant aircraft.

"Must be our air cover for the convoy," Verna said. Soon we could see several planes flying in and out of the clouds over the ships behind us, and flashes of antiaircraft fire.

Then, as we watched in horror, the bright flash of an exploding bomb lit one of the ships under the planes, followed a few seconds later by a hollow boom. We saw the ship slowly upending, heading downward, and heard the belated sounds of distant antiaircraft guns searching for a target in the clouds.

We wanted desperately to see the flash of the plane being hit, but it escaped into the nearby clouds, unharmed.

A voice jolted us out of our trance: "What in *hell* are you doing here?" A ship's officer ran toward us from the fore part of the ship. "That's all the damn Germans need is to know we've got women aboard and we'll be the next one under! Now, get your rear ends back to your cabins—on the triple double, and STAY THERE!"

"How in the world could anyone tell if we were men or women, even up close, with all this gear on?" whispered Verna. But we triple-doubled back to our closets, and stayed there.

Lying in our bunks a few seconds later, we heard distant bursts of gunfire and bombs. Sally, the only one who could peek out our porthole from her bunk, reported that we were in fog. Evidently, our ship had hidden in the nearest fogbank. Before long, all was quiet again. Just the creaking of the ship and the sloshing of the waves.

Hours went slowly by. It was late afternoon when we finally arrived in the harbor at Le Havre. We quickly got the order to disembark. Gathering up our possessions and shouldering our heavy duffel bags, we lined up on the deck. The LST backed up to within 150 feet of the beach and let down its rear ramp. Loaded down with all our gear, we waded ashore onto the sandy beach of Normandy, a lovely place had it been good weather, and if there had been no shot-up army equipment, sunken boats, and ruined docks. Abandoned concrete German gun emplacements still loomed menacingly from the top of the cliffs. It was impossible not to imagine the dread our troops felt months earlier when they landed there in the face of those guns pouring lead down on them as they stumbled through the surf and the monstrous shell holes. We tried not to remember that we had been warned to be careful from now on about possible leftover German snipers.

An army truck met us at the beach and took our duffel bags up the cliffs to a chateau that had recently been used by the

Germans. We were given a quick, cold C-ration supper at the army camp at the base of the upper cliffs, then marched up the narrow, muddy, slippery side-hill road to a chateau.

It sounds so glamorous, living in a real French chateau! All I can say is that it had a good roof and was dry inside. The Germans had stripped the once-lovely rooms of everything, ruining the walls and oak floors. There was only one bathroom, which did not work most of the time. And no heat. We slept on the floor in our sleeping bags and washed in dabs of water in our helmets.

For over a week we waited for transportation to Charleroi (pronounced Shar-le-rwah), Belgium, and the Ninth Air Force HQ. Three times a day we were marched back down the cliff for meals, and the rest of the time we cleaned our boots, cleaned the chateau, and watched the steady snow or rain. We never saw any local people, and the GIs were too involved in the war for the usual friendliness and banter. We began to feel totally forgotten and isolated. We were told that more men had been killed in the bitter fighting in Normandy after D-day than on D-day itself because of leftover German land mines and booby traps and the remaining pockets of German resistance in northern France.

Then, very early one miserably cold morning, two battered army trucks, their back ends covered with canvas, rumbled up the muddy hill to our chateau. We were to head for Charleroi within ten minutes. One GI drove each truck, while one armed soldier stood next to him with head, arms, and machine gun thrust through a hole in the truck roof.

We squeezed into the benches along the sides of the truck so tightly we couldn't possibly move a foot or an arm. With our bags piled in the middle aisle on top of our feet, off we went toward Belgium. The roads were rough. It was snowing. The wind was blowing. Little snowdrifts formed on us and our gear, no matter how tightly we tried to tie the flaps at the back of the trucks. We pitied the poor GIs with their heads outside. At first, we tried to sing to keep our spirits up, but were told to keep quiet so it would not be obvious that there were American women in these trucks. No one was sure where the front lines were at the moment.

Driving was slow. It must have been about eight that night when we drove into an army field camp for supper. Someone had called ahead and warned them that we were coming, so they had prepared for us as best they could. GIs took to the woods when nature demanded, but for us they had set up a large tent in the mud and snow at the edge of their area. No toilets: just a big empty tent.

In the middle of camp were big kettles with some leftover mutton stew (one of the horrors of wartime cuisine). By now this gourmet meal was lukewarm and thick with grease, but we ate it. We washed our mess kits in the prescribed two waters, one with soap and one with disinfectant. Fires under these big kettles had burned low, so the water was almost cold. The mutton fat from the company's supper dishes was congealing at least four inches thick on top of both kettles, but we washed our mess kits in these kettles according to army rules, even though they came out much greasier than they went in.

Then, back to our trucks for more hours of wind, snow, darkness, and complete immobility as we crept along through northern France. A couple of the girls were having their monthly periods, so we tried to give them the more protected places in the middle, but it didn't help much. There was no escaping the icy wind and drifting snow, and there was no way to move around to restore circulation in our half-frozen bodies.

After several more hours of jolting slowly over rough, deserted roads with the truck's headlights hooded, we stopped near a crossroads for a break. By now we realized we were somewhere north of Paris, and that we had been lost for quite a while.

We saw the GIs poring over some maps in the truck cab as

they tried to locate our position. Suddenly the driver jumped down and called our captain over. "Get them back in the truck NOW! And be quiet about it! We're getting out of here *fast*! We're back of the German lines!"

In almost total blackness, we bumped along much faster for a while, but we didn't see anyone else on the road. The Germans never dreamed a bunch of American WAAFs could be in their midst on such a miserable night.

We were all numb with cold from lack of movement and exhaustion, but on and on we drove. Finally, after what seemed forever, the truck stopped. Someone lifted the flaps in back and said, "Welcome to Charleroi."

It was three o'clock in the morning, and Ninth Air Force HQ was not expecting us for several more days. We tumbled out of the truck on leaden legs and were taken into the mess hall in the old school building used for headquarters. Here we were given some ancient lukewarm tea and some dry bread and butter. Nothing was prepared for us, but here we were, only half alive.

After a bit of conferring, the officers decided the best they could do for us at the moment was to give us an empty classroom for the night. Gathering all our gear, we blindly followed our officers to a big, empty, unheated classroom with white marble floors. We unrolled our sleeping bags, took off our boots, and loosened our belts before rolling up our jackets for pillows and bedding down on that cold marble. We were so exhausted that the floor didn't even feel hard. "Lights off" an officer said, and flicked the switch.

No one said a word. We just lay there staring at the ceiling for several minutes. Then someone sobbed. A deep guttural sob. And suddenly every girl in that room was sobbing deep, gut-wrenching, soul-shaking sobs that seemed to come from nowhere, but which tore up the lengths of our bodies from the bottoms of our feet to our aching throats. There were no tears.

No sniffles. No words. Just great earth-shaking, uncontrollable sobs. It did not feel like crying. Just deep, tension-releasing sobs.

As suddenly as they started, the sobs stopped and everyone was asleep.

They let us sleep until 8:00 A.M. the next day, an unbelievable concession from our WAAF officers. No one mentioned the night before. In all the years since then, I have never heard anyone who was there mention those sobs.

CHARLEROI

It was our first morning in Belgium, and we were trying to choke down the standard breakfast: rubbery, awful-textured powdered eggs, stale bread, and more of that lukewarm, ancient tea, but we were hungry enough that morning to eat that lousy chow. (We didn't often eat breakfast while we were in Belgium—especially after drinking a few cups of greasy coffee with salt instead of sugar, thanks to some joker.)

"Atten-SHUN!" barked our C.O. Benches scraped noisily as we jumped to our feet.

"At ease, ladies," followed immediately as the local air force wing commander came into the mess hall.

"Let me welcome all of you to the Ninth Air Force headquarters in Charleroi, Belgium," he continued. "As you know, the Allied forces have been engaged in a battle for this area since mid-December when the Germans tried to reach Brussels and Antwerp through the Ardennes Forest in southeast Belgium, just east of here. It has been a very hard winter for everyone. This headquarters has been overworked and understaffed. Our Allied forces are now preparing to launch a major offensive to reach the Rhine River. So we are very glad to have you here to help relieve some of the pressure."

"Let me apologize for not being prepared for you, but we were not notified of your exact arrival time and did not expect you this soon." He went on to tell us that we would be living in a house several blocks away that members of the German army's women's auxiliary—the "Mädchen," as we called them—had occupied until a few weeks before. We would be eating in the mess hall at the headquarters.

After a few minor announcements about assignments, he startled us by observing that there was a chance that the German army might sweep back through this sector at any time. "The battle of the Bulge has not been finalized as yet. The situation is fluid. We must be prepared to evacuate the area within five minutes' notice, day or night. If you are told that we must leave, drop everything and climb into the next vehicle heading out. If, by chance, you are taken prisoners by the Germans, do not—I repeat, *do not*—let the Germans know that you have had any training whatsoever in firearms. You want to be classified as unarmed personnel. All you need to answer to any of their questions is your name, rank, and serial number. Now please be aware that we are truly glad to see you. If there is anything I or my staff can do to help you get settled in, please let me know."

"My girls won't need any help, sir," our super-GI captain said stiffly. "We can do anything men can do." These were her favorite answers to everything, and we resented the hell out of her attitude. Many times we needed, and would have welcomed, a little help. We were soldiers—but we were still women.

Our captain had the same unusual last name that my grandmother's family had, but I never mentioned to her the fact that we might be related because I disliked her so much.

After breakfast that morning, we marched five or six blocks to an attractive old three-story house that had once been surrounded by a very lovely walled-in backyard garden. The German Mädchen had obviously deserted the place on short notice, because the house was a dirty, nasty mess. There was no heat, and only a sporadic trickle of cold water from the taps in the two small bathrooms, one on the first floor and one in the basement. I was assigned a fourth-floor (attic) room with two of my friends, and we were given army cots to sleep on, with no mattresses. Then we set to work cleaning out the filth that was everywhere.

We scrubbed and mopped with a vengeance most of the day. That afternoon, I discovered one of my roommates vomiting in the bathroom. She had been assigned the repulsive job of cleaning a small basement closet just big enough to hold a toilet stool. The narrow path to the toilet led through twenty-to-thirty-inch-deep banks of old, used condoms piled high behind the stool and along the walls. We had heard rumors before about the low morals of the Mädchen. These Mädchen had obviously been very busy, but not always with office work.

Late that afternoon, the front doorbell rang. A very large, very proper British officer, replete with waxed moustache and swagger stick, announced to our captain in a cultured English accent that he was the British army liaison officer for the area and wished to welcome us. As he looked around at the dirty, bedraggled, exhausted girls and the cold, dreary house, he asked if everything was all right.

"Of course," snapped our captain.

"Do you have any heat?" he asked.

"No."

"Do you have hot water?"

"Just a little cold water now and then."

"Beds? Mattresses?"

"Army cots. No mattresses."

"Was this house cleaned and ready for you?"

"No."

He stood there for a minute, his face purpling, as he opened and closed his mouth a few times, then roared, "Madam! How could you subject your troops to such awful conditions when it is not necessary?" Each word got louder and more vehement, resounding through the entire house. "And especially young American ladies." His feet involuntarily stomped up and down.

"Good day, madam. My condolences to your troops." With that, he marched out the front door without a backward glance.

Within less than an hour, British soldiers arrived to fix the furnace and the plumbing (still no hot water, but at least an adequate stream of cold water). A couple of hours later, mattress covers filled with fresh straw were delivered to alleviate the discomfort of our bare army cots.

Bless the British army!

Charleroi was an industrial city in the southern part of Belgium. It must have been a pleasant place in peacetime, but we saw it at its worst. The southern end of town with its railroad terminal and industrial areas had been heavily bombed a number of times during the battle of Ardennes. Our headquarters was in the north-central part of town, a residential and small-business area.

Around the corner from our house in Charleroi was another lovely old home that had been leased by an army infantry unit to house their personnel on temporary duty in that area.

Shortly after we moved in, two sergeants from this company were billeted in that house while they worked as special envoys to the Ninth Air Force headquarters. Don was tall and thin, with a wry sense of humor and a perpetual grin. Casey was an Irishman from Kansas City with a twinkle in his eye.

Verna never got used to the damp cold of English and Belgian winters, so on the first good days of spring, she eagerly took advantage of a flat roof over the back of our house to lie in the warm sun. From his room, Don noticed her lying there and made motions to let her know he would like to come over to meet her.

Before many more days, Don and Verna, Casey and I, became a foursome. Don and Casey had a jeep available for their use, so we could take occasional drives around town and within a short distance outside the city limits (if the battle lines weren't too close). Jeeps were "known to the ends of the earth," rough-riding, with no protection from the weather, strictly utilitarian. Ernie Pyle, the war correspondent, called jeeps "a divine instrument of military locomotion—as faithful as a dog, as strong as a mule, and as agile as a goat." General Eisenhower said that the jeep, the Dakota, and the landing craft were the three items that won the war. One European carmaker said that jeeps were the only true American sports car. I just know it was sometimes fun to have a jeep available for riding around.

Don and Casey often invited us to their house for dinner because their rations were more generous than ours. They did their own cooking. They had no cookbooks, and neither was talented as a cook, but we always ate everything and enjoyed it. They were even able to trade with a local farmer to get a few eggs, and that was a real luxury! We hadn't seen eggs for many months, and they tasted wonderful. Casey even made us a cake one day. It turned out soggy and very peculiar looking, but it tasted sort of sweet, so we ate that, too.

(I have lost track of Casey, but Verna never wanted to be cold again, so she and Don settled in the Southwest after returning from Europe.)

POOR BELGIUM

By day two in Belgium, we were at our assigned jobs at the Ninth Air Force headquarters in Charleroi. The unit, under-staffed and behind on their work, needed our help badly. They really were glad to see us arrive.

My job as a cryptographic technician kept me busy coding and decoding secret messages to and from various U.S. Army Air Force, U.S. Army, and British units. We used a number of codes. Some were set on machines fairly quickly, but others had to be worked out manually and took more time. Messages were sent and received via teletype, radio, and armed messengers.

The code room staff included one WAAF (me), three enlisted men, and one WAAF officer (Lieutenant Mary Emerson). Soon we became a close-knit group, almost a family. We felt that our work was important, and the friendships and mutual respect that developed between us made our time there almost a pleasure.

The German codes had been broken earlier by an elite group of Allied cryptographers known as ULTRA, although it took the Germans some time to realize their communications had been compromised. Outdated British and American codes had to be revised and replaced constantly, and the corrections distributed to all units in our area, which included most of Belgium and Holland. Many times during those final battles of the war, American units would be overrun by the Germans or would be forced to evacuate an area in a hurry. Now and then the code lists would fall into enemy hands. Those compromised codes had to be changed immediately. When this happened, our staff members were sent out to each of our wings with replacement codes. Each of us was given a jeep, an armed driver, and precise orders about delivering the codes. These trips never took more than a day, and we were able to see a lot of Belgium and Holland.

GIs at these isolated units had not seen an American woman for months. As soon as our jeep drove into their area, word would spread quickly that a real, live American girl was in camp. Lines of soldiers would form on both sides of the road as we drove in. "Are you really an American?" "Where ya from, Corporal?" "Say something in American!"

I learned to grin at all of them and keep a fast line of banter going with the crowd as my driver and I dashed to find the unit code officer. As soon as the information was delivered, we were always invited to the mess hall for coffee or lunch. There is nothing that can do more for a girl's ego than having lunch with several hundred men, all vying for her attention. On the ride back to Charleroi it was hard to keep from crying as I remembered all those homesick guys craving some small reminder of home before many of them would be wounded or captured or killed.

American forces suffered just over a million casualties in World War II. About 76,000 of those occurred in the battle of the Bulge, with hundreds more captured or missing. But enemy casualties came to more than 100,000, with huge losses of tanks, aircraft, and other equipment that the Germans could no longer replace. Aided by the British Seventh and Thirtieth Corps, 600,000 American troops fought the finest German troops available—and won. I remember reading somewhere, probably in *Stars and Stripes*, that Churchill called this battle in the Ardennes Forest "the greatest American battle of the war." The Ardennes was wild, rough country, with deep ravines, broad rivers, and poor roads. The weather had been horrible, lots of snow, cold temperatures, and mud. A terrible, terrible winter in every way.

Among the American units in our area were the U.S. First Army under General Hodges, the Third Army under General Bradley, Patton's Fourth Armored Division, the Ninth Armored Division, the Eighty-second and 101st Airborne divisions, and the Third, Fifth, Seventh, Eighth, and Ninth Air Forces.

Once when I was being sent to supply new codes to one of our wings, the jeep assigned to me was driven by a sergeant. I liked him because he was a quiet, thoughtful person in his late twenties who could talk about something besides sex and drinking. It was a quiet summer morning, and the countryside was beautiful. We had driven for quite some time when he glanced at me quickly, then turned and looked away without answering my last question. After a moment of silence, he blurted, "Would you be interested in seeing something the Germans did before they left this area a month or so ago?"

"Sure." I was curious.

"You might be shocked. It's pretty bad," he warned.

"Oh, well. I've seen a lot of other pretty bad stuff," I said, not knowing this would be the beginning of years of nightmares.

We turned east off the quiet country road and drove up a narrow dirt trail for half a mile. At the top of a slight rise was a long, scraggly row of trees with a few people stooping over in the bright sunlight to see something. As we came nearer the top of the little hill, we could see that they were peering into a long trench, maybe 150 feet long. We walked the last few yards in silence before we were close enough to look down into the shallow trench, which was only three or four feet deep and about five feet wide. It was filled with bodies. Some had been removed already, but there must have been seventy-five or a hundred left. The stench of half-decomposed bodies filled the air.

As Allied troops advanced into Belgium, the sergeant explained, the Germans panicked. The group of POWs they were holding slowed down their retreat, so, instead of just leaving them behind, the Germans marched a whole group of them to the top of this little hill, made them dig the trench, and ordered them to stand at attention in front of it. The long line of people was then machine-gunned so they would tumble backward into the trench. They lay as they fell, some on top of one another. If a body was too tall for the trench, the legs had been broken and bent upwards over the body to make them fit in. There were men in uniform, Belgians, French, English, Americans, as well as civilians—men, women, and even children.

The army had identified most of the Americans, although some of their dog tags were missing. Other people were drifting in from all over Europe to try to identify loved ones. The bodies had not decomposed too much, so it was still possible to identify some of the people.

Horrified, I stared at the bodies. Then suddenly the broken legs were more than I could stand. I ran down the hill and was sick.

I did not know where this hilltop was. The sergeant and I

could never talk about it. But later I tentatively identified it as Malmédy (we pronounced it "MAL-muh-dee"), where hidden witnesses had watched the German SS troops kill prisoners of war in December 1944. I had nightmares about that quiet, sunlit hilltop and those broken legs for years after that.

Many of the Germans who perpetrated this monstrous, unnecessary foulness were buried at Bitburg, where President Reagan visited forty years later to honor them. He even asked us to forgive and forget, and to feel sorry for these poor, misled German boys. How can anyone forgive atrocities such as these?

It was almost always cold, dank, and rainy while we were in Belgium. That year spring came reluctantly and fleetingly. Everyday life was grim and full of struggles. Our house, as well as Headquarters, had practically no heat, so we wore as many layers of clothing as possible and worked with fingers stiffened by the cold.

Since we had no hot water in our house, it was necessary to go to the public baths—quite an experience. The baths were in the center of town in a huge old building reminiscent of early Roman baths. Efficiently run by Belgiques, the baths were always crowded with men and women seeking one of the few sources of hot water in the area. For a small fee, each customer received a clean towel and the choice of a tub or a shower, each in its own small cubicle.

I tried a tub bath . . . once! The Belgian woman attendant rather perfunctorily rinsed out the tub with cleaning powder and a brush, turned the warm water on, pulled shut the curtain over the door, and left. After lowering myself into the tub, I could feel a solid bed of gritty cleanser under me, and I had visions of all the other backsides which had recently been abraded in the same sandy spot. After that I always used the showers, which were quite satisfactory. And the hot water was sheer luxury!

On February 13 and 14, Dresden, one of the most beautiful

cities in Germany, was almost obliterated by American and British firebombs. As many as 135,000 civilian may have died in that one raid alone. All that month, and part of the next month, Leipzig and other German cities were bombed mercilessly by the Allies in some of the worst air raids of the war. Our code room worked night and day to keep up with all the secret messages necessary to these operations.

The first few months after we arrived in Belgium, the battle lines wavered back and forth across eastern Belgium and Germany as the Allies pushed toward Berlin. We could tell how close the fighting was and in which direction the armies were moving by watching the lines of refugees that continually trudged back and forth through town.

The stream of blank-eyed, weary remnants of people dragging themselves slowly from nothing to nowhere seemed neverending. Clad in rags, with broken-down shoes or rags on their feet, they carried everything they had left in this world in packs on their backs or on wobbly wheeled carts or wagons. They had no homes, no jobs, no money, little food, no shelter—many with no families left alive, no place to go—their past destroyed, no future in sight. Watching these sad wrecks of people broke our hearts. Skinny, starved children, cripples, and sick old people close to death were perched atop cartloads pushed slowly along by their exhausted, emaciated relatives. Nobody talked. No children played or laughed. Nobody smiled. There was no eye contact, nor signs of recognition of what they saw or where they were. Where they slept or what they ate remained a mystery to us. Their lives were a ceaseless putting of one foot in front of the other, with no hoping, nor thinking, nor trying to feel. Just flight from the horrors behind them to the emptiness ahead. An existence on the bare edge of oblivion. If the front lines were close, the refugees headed westward toward France and away from Germany. Then, after the Allies began to get closer to Berlin, thinner lines headed back toward homes and families in the East . . . or what was left of them.

The Belgian people could do little to help the refugees. Under German occupation there had been too much bombing and too much looting for too long. They were lucky to have the barest minimum of food and shelter for themselves, with none to spare for refugees. There was also deep distrust of the refugees because many German soldiers had been discovered in the area disguised as refugees, aiming toward sabotage and spying. Many security checks were set up by the U.S. Army to ferret out these spies, but no one could know how many went undiscovered.

Our headquarters cooks were horrified each time they had to take a truckload of kitchen garbage to the dumps. Because our food supplies were limited, few leftovers remained from our mess, but when the cooks emptied their garbage cans from the back of a truck at the dump, a crowd of people always waited to grab anything remotely edible. People with their cups and pans, people who had once been well off, fought to get right under the garbage being spilled out so they could be sure to get something to eat. Every little bone or piece of wilted vegetable was treasured. A moldy loaf of bread could cause a vicious, clawing fight. Nobody worried about getting covered with kitchen slops. Clothes and faces could be washed later. Now was the time to get what you could, one way or another. "Now *that's* real hunger. Those people are really desperate," one cook told me, trying to hide his emotion. "Makes you want to cry," he added softly, looking away.

One day several of us toured a nearby steel plant. Most Belgian people were wary and secretive, but the Belgian man conducting the tour told us proudly that most of the workers ("the *real* Belgians," he said with a wink) had managed to slow production down almost to a standstill under the Germans by faked illnesses, unaccidental accidents, and pretended shortages. Now they were trying hard to get their production back up again in spite of outdated machinery and real material shortages. Skilled labor was at a premium because so many workers had been killed or imprisoned by the Germans, many in retaliation for sabotage.

On the outskirts of Charleroi the Germans had set up a prison camp for male and female Russian soldiers captured in east Germany. In the Wehrmacht's retreat, the camp had been abandoned by the Germans. Inmates of this camp felt very lucky because they had not been shot as so many other prisoners had been. Their war was over for the moment, and they were free to come and go as they pleased. They remained at the camp, fed by the Americans, until the war in eastern Germany would end and they could be sent home. Elated by the impending Allied victory, they marched through the streets daily, singing heartily—strong women and joyous men, happy to be alive, and proud to be Russian. The Russians lost many millions dead in World War II, with many, many more millions of civilian casualties, and these soldiers were filled with bitterness, looking forward to the revenge they would inflict on the German people.

At night many of these Russians frequented the few local bars to drink vodka and sing. It fascinated me to watch them down one drinking glass full of vodka after another after another . . . with no apparent effects. Once in a while, some foolish American would try to drink with them. "Bottoms up," the Russians grinned. Very few Americans could finish a second glass without passing out cold.

Another local bar added to my sex education one night. My date and I had gone there because they had music (sort of) to dance to. As I watched the other dancers I became confused.

"Ken," I whispered across the table. "See those two women dancing together? I think that dark-haired one is flirting with you."

"Oh, no!" he grinned. "It's flirting with *you*."

We left immediately, with Ken laughing all the way. "I thought you knew what kind of a place that was," he chortled.

I occasionally went out with another GI who belonged to an army headquarters unit with a bakery attached. We always ended the evening with a visit to his buddies, the bakers. That fresh-baked, crusty, fragrant bread with real butter melting slowly down into it! Heaven! The most delightful food I had eaten in what seemed forever.

Because a real danger from snipers or German sympathizers still existed in the area, we could not go outside the main part of town unless we had special permission. The Belgian people had been so battered by the occupation that we had little contact with any of them. They showed us little friendliness. We seldom saw or heard children, and local residents hurried past us on the streets with eyes averted. They had learned to be as inconspicuous as possible under German rule. Even dogs and cats seemed to have disappeared.

The cold, soggy, dreary, damp winter that caused so much misery for the soldiers fighting this war seemed to last forever. But finally, the sun fought through the clouds, the old dirty snow melted, and grass and trees started to green again. It was pleasant to have the streets and fields dry once more, even though bombed-out buildings and roads became uglier and more visible.

After the fighting front had moved into Germany, I received a phone call from Brussels. My cousin Lorraine's husband, Fred Reynolds, said his company would be in Brussels for a few days and asked me to come up for a visit if I could. I scurried around and found that a courier from our headquarters was going to Brussels the next day and could give me a ride. Proper permissions were granted, and off I went.

Fred and I spent the day exchanging news from home and walking about the old city. It was the only time I was able to be in that area, so I really enjoyed the day. Of course, we only saw the center of the city, but I found it very impressive and beautiful, even in wartime. And of course we were amused by the famous little statue of the peeing boy. The courier truck left for Charleroi at 4:00 P.M., so it was a short visit.

This visit with Fred was the only time I ever saw someone I knew from home while in the ETO.

Another summer evening I shall always remember seemed like a theater production. A young army lieutenant I met in Charleroi in the code room invited me to dinner at his headquarters several miles away in the countryside. He called for me in his jeep after work and took me to one of the loveliest chateaux I have ever seen. A long lane of trees led up through beautiful lawns and topiary gardens to the chateau. Nothing seemed to have been touched by war or neglect.

The other unit personnel stationed there had gone to a party somewhere and my friend was left in charge. Servants served us dinner by candlelight in a huge, vaulted, wood-paneled dining room. And, of course, there was champagne.

After dinner we went outside to dance by the light of the summer moon. A phonograph sitting on one of the low side walls of a stone terrace provided soft music, and the gentle breeze held the aroma of many flowers. It was an enchanted night! I could have danced all night. But Cinderella had to be home by ten, so it all ended much too soon. It was so lovely while it lasted!

THE FINAL DAYS OF THE WAR

So many important events happened so fast while we were in Belgium! After the terrible winter in the Ardennes (the battle of the Bulge), the Allies had finally been able to push the German forces back into Germany and to end the awful conflict.

About the time we arrived in Belgium, in mid-February 1945, Allied bombing had made shambles of the German railroads, air force installations, and munitions plants. Germany was on its knees, short of both raw materials and manufactured goods.

Their gas, power, water, and rail systems were in chaos. Supplies of petrol and other fuels were almost exhausted. And their communications systems were so disorganized as to be practically useless.

From the *Stars and Stripes*, we heard nearly every day of major new battles. Letters from home listed casualties we knew: *So and so died in the Pacific . . . on Okinawa . . . in Italy . . . .* Such letters kept us aware that the people at home were as worried about all these grave battles as we were. Here are a few of the many developments we heard of:

On February 19, U.S. forces began the assault on Iwo Jima—the terrible fighting was not over until March 16.

On February 26, there were major incendiary attacks on Tokyo.

On March 7, the Allies seized the Remagen bridge over the Rhine and breached the last major barrier between U.S forces and Berlin.

On March 22, there were a number of crossings of the Rhine, including Patton's tank corps.

The next day, March 23, there were many more crossings, including Montgomery and his British troops.

On April 1, the United States started the assault on Okinawa.

A few weeks later, in April, we heard that the Canadian forces were facing some of the toughest resistance in this final stage of the war near Arnhem in northern Holland.

On April 12, 1945, President Franklin Roosevelt died. His death was a great shock to American troops. A truly great leader, he represented the spirit of our country to everyone. He was our president, our commander in chief, and a father figure all rolled into one. Many unashamed tears were shed that day. "I felt as if I knew him. I felt as if he knew me. And I felt as if he liked me" was heard more than once.

April 16, the U.S. Seventh Army reached Nürnberg in Germany.

April 21, U.S. troops reached the outskirts of Berlin on the west, and the Red Army arrived at the eastern edge of that city.

On April 25, the American and Red armies met at the River Elbe.

April 29, German armies in Italy surrendered.

Hitler died the next day, April 30!

On May 2, 1945, Soviet forces completed the capture of Berlin.

May 4, 1945, German troops in the Netherlands, Denmark, and northwest Germany surrendered.

And at 1:41 A.M. Central European Time on the seventh of May, the Germans surrendered at Reims. President Truman proclaimed May 8 as V-E Day.

When word of the surrender reached us, I remember no big parties or wild celebrations. We were too close to the war for that. Instead, we felt grief for all our friends and loved ones who had died in this horrible war. We felt deep pity for the people of Europe, with their broken cities and families, who now had to rebuild their lives and countries with the little or nothing available to them.

We also felt both proud and humble about our own part in this war. Proud of the courageous GIs who had risked their lives (or lost them) in a foreign country for principles we could all understand. Humble, because we had also seen the bravery and sacrifice of the fighting men of Europe—and the fighting civilians: men, women, and children.

Probably the words we heard the most often that day were "Now we can go home!" Everyone had his or her own private dream of seeing loved people, places, things again, and not-so-private fantasies of favorite foods to be gorged on as soon as U.S. shores were reached. "Gonna get me all the eggs and ice cream I can hold" was always accompanied by a grin from ear to ear.

Several weeks later, a well-planned and impressive "Victoire-Paix" Day parade was held in Charleroi. Marching together

were troops of all the Allies: American, British, Scots Highlanders, French, Canadian, Belgian, Russian, Australian. There
were war-battered tanks, flag-draped jeeps, and every type of
army vehicle—all filled with GIs and officers and local officials.
And there was magnificent air cover that day to add to the general uproar. American units received great ovations from the
crowds lining the streets. It was an exciting day!

Our WAC company (sharp looking in our dress uniforms, if
I may say so!) marched toward the front, so we were able to see
a lot of the rest of the several-miles-long parade. Bands from
various units and countries joyfully played their favorite marching songs, including Scottish bagpipers, and the streets were
lined with huge crowds waving all the various Allied flags
and cheering madly. It was an amazing parade. Everyone was
elated because the war was over, and sad at remembrance of
comrades not there.

There were only three small groups of women marching in
this parade that I knew about: some Russian women soldiers,
a group of nurses, and our small WAC unit.

That evening a fireworks display was held in a downtown
square, and several of us walked down to watch it. The square
was packed with thousands of people, so we were able to squeeze
only a short way into the crowd. Local dignitaries gave speeches,
and then the fireworks started. I was horrified to see that they
were not being shot up high enough and were coming down on
the crowd. "Let's get out of here," I gasped to my friends. We
were jammed in so tightly that if anyone had fainted, they could
not have fallen down. It was very difficult, but we banded together and finally managed to get out. It was one of the most
frightening moments of the war for me. I remembered hearing about a similar incident in Paris a few years before where a
large number of people had been trampled to death when a
dense crowd panicked as fireworks rained down on them.

After the parade, we began to realize that the war was really
over at last. Now our main topic of conversation was the point

system. One point for every month in service, extra points for overseas duty or if you were married or pregnant, and those with the most points would get to go home first!

IN AND OUT OF HOSPITALS

Our Charleroi diet was far from gourmet. Since most available cargo space on incoming planes or ships was needed for battleground supplies, food shipments were limited to basic necessities. We ate a lot of C rations, concentrated foods that allowed a whole meal to be packed into a small box for easy carrying in the field. There was usually a can of stew or Spam, some cookies, a chocolate bar, cigarettes, a small pack of toilet paper, and a serving-size packet of instant coffee, maybe some lemonade powder. Since I didn't smoke, I was always very popular until my cigarettes were given away.

Our mess hall in the HQ building was run by army personnel. One thing was for sure: These cooks could never make their living as cooks in civilian life, and not having proper supplies made their products even worse.

A typical breakfast consisted of powdered eggs, stale toast with stale canned butter or white margarine, powdered milk, and coffee or tea that had been made the night before in huge kettles and steeped all night. They added sugar to the tea or coffee, and it was horrible battery-acid stuff. We had to walk several blocks to the mess hall for this feast through snow and mud, so usually we skipped breakfast and shared cookies or a candy bar from home. At first, we went over to the mess hall for some coffee, but after the aforementioned joker put salt instead of sugar into the brew a few times, we decided the trip through the snow and mud just wasn't worth the bother. The men said this coffee was good for shaving because at least it was hot.

Lunch and supper seemed to alternate between C rations and mutton stew. The Australians had sent shiploads of mutton to the ETO, and it was awful. Sheep meat, we called it: old, tough, stringy, strong-smelling, even stronger-tasting, with lots and lots of mutton fat that coated your teeth and mouth and throat.

There were no fresh vegetables, fruits, or eggs, no fresh dairy products, no fresh meats. We ate because we had to, not because the food tasted good. Everyone's uniforms became sizes too large from such a poor diet. Surprisingly, there was not as much griping about our meals as one might expect. Everyone realized the logistics problems involved, and besides we were getting used to army food by then. In England we had been able to find edible food locally, but in Belgium food supplies were too scarce to support restaurants. The local people were lucky to find enough food to keep themselves and their families alive.

After a few months in Belgium, I began to have digestive problems. I could not keep the army food down, partly due to the food itself, and partly because of stress. As a result, I was sent to various army hospitals during the last few months I was in Belgium to try to find a cure for my problems.

One hospital stay was somewhere near Namur in an old castle high on a rocky point overlooking a broad valley. During the week I was there, I spent many hours wandering along the ramparts enjoying the view.

A few weeks later, I was sent to a hospital in Luxembourg for another week of tests. Many of the patients there were from General Patton's tank battalions, which had only recently suffered a great many casualties as they fought through Germany. There were burn patients, amputees, everything mixed together.

"Yeah, I'm one of Patton's tank commanders," one soldier told me as he picked invisible butterflies out of the air and admired them as they sat on his hand. "See this one?" he asked. "Ever see such pretty colors?"

"Gorgeous," I agreed, trying to look as if I saw something.

"Damn General Patton to hell," he continued in a monotone. "He sent a whole battalion of our tanks right down the center of that field outside of Remagen. Damn him. *Damn* him!

He *could* have let us go around the edges. He knew . . . we *all* knew . . . that field was heavily mined."

"What happened?" I asked softly.

His eyes glazed as he looked off somewhere far beyond me. "We all got blown to bloody hell. I'm the only one left of my tank crew. They all burned to a crisp behind me after I got blown out. Tanks exploding, burning all around that field. Men screaming, burning, blown apart."

He was watching that battlefield again in full, deadly color, his face pale and distorted, his eyes glassy.

Maybe I'd better leave him alone. Or maybe I should call an orderly, I thought.

Then, after a minute, he continued in a flat, dead voice. "The bastard should have let us go around the edge of that field instead of ordering us straight down the middle. He knew what would happen to us. He *knew*. But people don't mean nothin' to him, just as long as *he* looks good for the newspapers." He paused another moment, then, almost in a whisper, as he stared into space: "I hope he rots in hell forever."

As quietly as I could, I walked away, even though I knew he was not seeing or hearing me just then. An hour later I saw him again, happily catching his butterflies. "Got a big one this time," he chortled.

"Ah, Jimmy. You're braggin'," said one of the patients who was his buddy. "That there's just a dirty old moth." And the two of them wandered off across the grass, arguing about the colors of the nonexistent bugs they both saw.

Jimmy was from Florida and often showed me pictures of his beautiful, suntanned, blonde fiancée, whom he was looking forward to marrying as soon as he got home—if he could stay alive that long. Within days after I arrived at the hospital, he was sent back to his unit in spite of his problems. He was needed because his company was engaged in heavy fighting as they headed toward Berlin.

In early May 1945, toward the end of my time in Belgium,

I spent a fortnight in an army hospital on the southeast edge of Paris. The huge old building overlooked a large field filled with tents and guards: It was a POW camp for captured German soldiers. The weather was fine just then, and in the evenings we could hear the German prisoners singing as they sat around their campfires. Many of their songs were familiar to us, many of them were Nazi army songs, many old German folksongs. One of their favorites, which they usually sang just before going to bed, was "Lili Marlene." The sad, sweet melody sung softly by hundreds of young German men drifted across to our hospital windows. Listening to it, we couldn't help thinking about the sadness and uselessness of war, wishing we could just go home to our families and forget it all.

None of my hospital visits did anything to cure my stomach problems. However, as soon as I returned home to Iowa, I visited our old family doctor. After an examination and some questions, he handed me some pills and said, "Nothing wrong with you but plain old nervous stomach. Take one of these pills with every meal and you'll feel better soon."

And he was right. Odd that none of those army doctors could ever understand how an awful diet, bombings, poor living conditions, and long hours of stressful work could give one a spastic stomach.

THE LOOS AND PISSERIES OF EUROPE

This story of my years in Europe during World War II would not be complete without at least a short chapter about the rest rooms we encountered along the way. In their various forms, they were amazing and amusing.

Mention has already been made of the loo in the headquarters building at Bushey, Herts, England, with its carefully painted cabbage roses outside and inside the various facilities, and the chain hanging from the ceiling to flush.

The chateau in Le Havre had regular (i.e., American-type)

appliances, but nothing worked well and there was only one tiny bathroom for the whole place.

The bare tent we were allowed to use on our way to Charleroi was also an experience, but one we did not want to repeat.

The toilet in the WAC billet in Charleroi was not unusual in itself—only in the piles of used condoms surrounding it.

And then there were the urinals (pissoirs, or as the GIs called them, "pisseries") on every other corner in the French, Dutch, and Belgian towns. These small buildings had no windows on three sides, but on the fourth, or front, side had doors at both ends with the stalls between. The patrons could watch the passersby through the space across the front at eye level. "I don't mind those guys staring at us as we go by," Verna said one day, "but it's sort of a shock to have them wave at us one-handed." Despite the availability of these facilities, many men didn't bother to use them but instead aimed at the nearest lamppost or wall. Young children were allowed to defecate in the gutters anywhere.

After the seemingly endless winter that year in Belgium and Holland, spring finally arrived. I understood at last why I had heard stories all my life about the immaculate Dutch housewives who scrubbed their front walks each day. It was very disillusioning to find out they had to do this because the old urine deposited there smelled so awful on those first warm days.

Restrooms at bars or restaurants were often a real adventure. Frequently there would be only one room, with male and female patrons using adjacent toilet stools with no walls or curtains between. As they attended to their business, they held pleasant conversations about the weather or the awful service at the bars since the war. To American WACs, this system was most embarrassing. Europeans were always very amused when we insisted that a GI stand guard at the door while we were inside so we could have a little privacy.

The toilet that baffled me the most was at a small country inn somewhere in northern France, where we stopped on our way home. There was a small, bare room, with no water or sink—only one board missing in the middle of the floor. We debated over which way to approach it, frontward or backward. And needless to say, it smelled awful.

Toilet paper was nonexistent in these public restrooms, and the sanitation in almost all of them was minimal, to say the least. Ancient stenches, flies, crawling things, and infinite layers of filth made us yearn for even the worst of American facilities. In my opinion, one of our country's greatest assets is our insistence on cleanliness and usability in these necessary rooms.

I LOVED PARIS IN THAT SPRINGTIME

Life in Belgium in early 1945 was grim, but the army made a special effort to give us leave time to relieve the stress. We were encouraged to travel to more peaceful parts of Europe on our time off and could take advantage of empty seats on planes to Orly airfield outside of Paris or to the Riviera.

All my life I had read stories about Paris: its romance and history, its gaiety and sophistication, its beauty and art. So I was delighted to be able to spend several wonderful weekends exploring this marvelous city. Even in wartime, and so soon after German occupation, it lived up to my dreams.

A famous old hotel in the middle of Paris had been converted into quarters for U.S. personnel on leave. It was close to the main shopping district, so we spent hours just window shopping at the world-famous couturier shops, parfum houses, and jewelers. On our return to Belgium, we always had well-stocked bags, mostly filled with the best French perfumes . . . enough to last for years.

In England we had been disappointed that the best art had been hidden away for safety during the war; the same was true in France. A few treasures had been returned to the galleries following the occupation, but most of the best works were still hidden.

Despite this, we managed to see a lot of Paris and to fall in love with that fascinating, beautiful city with its friendly, life-loving people.

My friends and I spent many days wandering the streets of Paris and staring in awe at the famous buildings and sights we had read about. We climbed to the top of the Sacré Coeur Cathedral for a marvelous view of the whole city, gazed upward in wonder at the Notre Dame Cathedral, wandered through Montmarte and down the Champs Elysées, ambled along the River Seine admiring the artists and their works, strolled through Pigalle and Moulin Rouge, and gasped at the wild crazy Paris traffic with its bicycle taxicabs and other vehicles all honking continuously as they drove full speed ahead!

We spent long hours browsing through as many small shops as we could find, stopping now and then for coffee or wine at sidewalk cafés. We were impressed by the eternal flame under the Arc de Triomphe and the massive old Opera House. Because it was still being used as a military communication center, the Eiffel Tower was off-limits to us, but we wandered around its base, getting cricks in our necks from looking up at it for so long.

After being in the service this long, I thought I had learned a lot. I was no longer the naive Montana ranch girl who had enlisted what seemed a long time ago . . . but I hadn't learned everything.

As Verna and I planned our first trip to Paris, one of the GIs in our HQ asked me if I would do him a favor since he could not get to Paris right then.

"Would you buy me some postcards?" he asked.

"Why, sure," I answered, unsuspectingly.

"Well," he continued, "everyone who goes to Paris *must*

see the stage show at the Folies Bergère. It's really good, and they have some great postcards on sale there in the lobby. I'll give you the money to buy me a couple sets, if you will."

"Okay," I answered, wondering at his rather sly grin.

So one of our first nights in Paris, we went to the Folies. To a Montana ranch girl, it was quite an eye-opener. The talent and the acts were excellent, with great music and wonderful stage sets and beautiful costumes. Except that none of the female entertainers wore anything above the waist! Their headgear was elaborate, their skirts and costumes were gorgeous—but no bras in sight. To me, in the 1940s, that was shocking.

I really was not expecting this, and I am sure the glow from my beet-red face lighted up half the theater. And then an odd thing happened: After about fifteen minutes all those bare breasts became commonplace. After our attention to those naked chests waned a bit, we began to watch the show itself, and to delight in how good it really was.

At intermission we went to the lobby where the show girls came out to sit with male patrons for a drink. Refreshments and souvenirs were for sale.

"You're not really going to buy some of those bare boob cards, are you?" whispered Verna.

"Of course I am," I answered stubbornly. "I promised Vic I would, and I'm not going to give him a chance to laugh at me because I lost my nerve, darn him anyway!"

So after carefully looking around to be sure no one in the lobby knew me, I bought *three* sets of the cards, two for Vic and the other set to show him I had a set, too! Later, I resold them to another GI for a tidy profit.

On another very special day in Paris, Helen and I started off early from our hotel. It was the first sunshiny day of early spring. The birds were singing, the grass was turning green, trees were budding, the breeze was soft and scented. People's faces wore unaccustomed smiles. The occupation was over, the war had almost ended, and that awful winter of 1944–1945 was finally breaking up. Life was looking much brighter.

As we wandered through a large open-air marketplace near the Notre Dame, I suddenly felt a tap on my shoulder. Turning, I saw a well-dressed, middle-aged Frenchman beaming at me.

"Ze américaines ma'amselles! We zank you. Come!" Gently he took my arm and led us to a nearby flower booth where an old lady was selling branches of yellow mimosa fresh from the south of France. The French gentleman purchased two huge armloads of these lovely blooms, presented them to us with a bow, smiled, kissed our hands, and disappeared into the crowd with a friendly wave.

Overwhelmed, we floated off on cloud nine with our armloads of gorgeous yellow mimosa. A younger Frenchman carrying a camera stopped us. In halting English he asked if we would like to have our pictures taken with our flowers. "Or much better, I take you to many beautiful places in Paris and take your pictures there for souvenir." The price he quoted was minimal, so we agreed. This was, indeed, an enchanted day.

Yves, our photographer, took dozens of pictures of us in all the usual tourist spots, as well as in parts of Paris we had never seen before. He was witty and charming and fun, and the blissful mood we were in because of the flowers deepened as the day passed. We smiled at everyone, and everyone smiled back at us, even the blue-haired ladies of the night. By five that afternoon we returned to our hotel for a delicious French dinner, completing an unforgettable Parisian day.

The next day a famous Paris designer sent two complimentary tickets for his yearly fashion show to our hotel, and Helen and I were lucky enough to receive them. As we sat there in the salon that afternoon, surrounded by fashion experts and buyers from around the world, sipping complimentary champagne, we tried very hard to look dignified, hoping no one could notice how scared and ill at ease we really were in such so-phisticated, worldly company. But it was such fun!

It was surprising how well we communicated with the French people, although few of us knew their language. Between an abundance of gestures and smiles, a little knowledge of English on their part, and a few standard phrases we picked up here and there, we managed quite well. "Merci beaucoup" helped a lot. Of course, GIs claimed their favorite French phrase was "Couchez avec moi?"

A few weeks later, Yves, true to his word, sent each of us an album of excellent pictures of our day in Paris.

THE RIVIERA

Late in July near the end of my time in Belgium, I was thrilled to be given the rare chance to spend a week on the French Riv-iera. I flew down to Nice on an army plane that followed the Rhône River Valley and skirted the western edges of the Alps, whose magnificent snow-covered peaks were impressive in the late afternoon sunlight.

A very old resort town, Nice curls protectively around a half moon of a bay on the French Riviera. This bay is on the Côte d'Azur, which is well-named for the vivid blue of the sea on that coast. The Riviera is famous for its year-round mild cli-mate, its sunshine, and the clear turquoise blue of the Mediter-ranean on that coast. For thousands of years, people from all over the world have flocked there to enjoy their leisure time.

A picturesque little old hotel on one of the hills back of the harbor at Nice housed female military personnel on leave from all over Europe. We had to be at the hotel for bedcheck by the sergeant in charge each night at midnight. (It was still the army!) But the rest of the time was our own to spend as we pleased in this wonderful place. And it was such a relief to be in a town that had not been bombed!

When our plane landed at the army air force airport southwest of Nice, we were greeted by a very handsome staff sergeant named Dan, who was detailed to drive the four army women on our plane to the hotel. On the way up the hill he asked me if I would like to go out to dinner and see some of the local night spots that evening. It sounded like fun, so as soon as I found my room and unpacked, off we went. Dan had taken the jeep back to the base and returned on the local commuter bus, but he had reserved a horse-drawn carriage for the evening. The clip-clop of the horses' hooves, the myriad smells of the sea and the masses of flowers in bloom everywhere, the overwhelming scent of night-blooming jasmine, the brilliant moon, all helped to set a most romantic mood.

The next morning, Dan came to the hotel with the news that he had been able to talk his CO into letting him take leave time for the week I would be there. Thus began a whirlwind romance and an unforgettable leave.

Dan was witty and fun to be with, and he devoted his week to helping me enjoy the Riviera and forget the war.

We spent long, sunny days on the Mediterranean beaches swimming or splashing around the harbor on paddleboats. Dan was well tanned from being stationed in Nice, but after cloudy, cold England and Belgium, my pale skin soon acquired a sunburn.

We had fun exploring Nice and the area. Remnants of ancient Roman aqueducts were still intact in places, and we picnicked among the ruins.

A tour in the countryside north of Nice through fields of flowers whose petals form the bases for the world-famous French perfumes taught us a little about the complicated business of making perfume.

One particularly fine day, Dan made arrangements for us to drive east along the coast to Monte Carlo and on into northern Italy. The casinos at Monte Carlo were off-limits to army personnel, but we were able to do a lot of sight-seeing through the narrow, winding, hilly streets in the tiny city-country. The well-protected harbor was filled with various small craft, even though it was wartime. Most of them were fishing boats, but there were also a number of yachts and private boats tied up at the docks. Fishermen mending their nets lined the beaches. Most of them were old men, since so many of the younger men had gone to war or had been killed.

Later we drove on to San Remo in northern Italy. No problems at the border because we were American and the war was still on. San Remo was a poor, small, hot, dry, dusty, sun-baked town on the beach that still managed to have a charm all its own. I was fascinated by the differences in people, architecture, and even scenery and climate between this place and Nice. The two towns were not far apart, yet it was evident that they were in two separate countries, two different worlds.

Back in Nice, evenings were filled with leisurely dinners at fine restaurants where imaginative French chefs managed to serve up wonderful meals despite wartime food shortages. There was lots of wine and dancing and laughter and fun. And before we could believe it, the week was almost over.

That last morning I enjoyed the services of the huge German masseuse who came around early each day at the hotel to rub away sore muscles and any leftover tensions. She never smiled as she rubbed and pounded and pushed—she really worked us over. After a long, leisurely, warm shower—so different from the public showers of Charleroi—I went downstairs to meet Dan for a pink champagne breakfast before the plane took off at noon.

Had my leave been a few days longer, Dan and I would probably have been married in Nice. As it was, we missed each other for a while and wrote often, but it was not long before we both were scheduled to go home. Without too much pain, we agreed that it had been a "shipboard" romance and that it had sure been lots of fun while it lasted. It would be something both of us would always remember—and always with a smile.

4

GERMANY

MY LAST DAYS IN EUROPE

The beat-up old Mitchell B-25 bomber that had been converted to a troop transport jounced and lurched through the rough air over the northern foothills of the Alps.

"You look a mite green," the GI sitting next to me said, laughing.

Well, I felt *worse* than green. Never before had I been carsick or seasick or airsick. But this morning I was also suffering from a bit of hangover, and my stomach was objecting strenuously to such abuse. The cold, the noise, the bouncing and vibration of the plane, and the uncomfortable parachutes strapped on our backs did nothing to help my problem.

I was on my way to Nürnberg in southern Germany in this war-weary plane. Its insides had been cleared out and benches built along each side wall for passengers. None of us knew why we had been chosen for transfer to the Ninth Air Force in Germany, although I presumed that I had been chosen because of my knowledge and experience with cryptography. But in Nürnberg I was assigned to a routine office typing job that had nothing to do with cryptography.

The night before leaving for Germany, the other members of my company in Belgium and assorted GIs had thrown a farewell party for me at a local bar and dance hall in Charleroi. Since most of us had earned nearly enough service points to go home, we knew that we probably would never see each other again. It had been quite a party: lots of drinks, fun, reminiscing, sentimental good-byes. But this morning I was regretting all those extra farewell drinks and those late-hour good-byes.

Nürnberg had been captured by American forces in mid-April 1945. It had been chosen as the site of the trials of Nazi war criminals, and preparation for the trials were in full swing.

On arrival in Nürnberg, we were billeted in barracks just west of the city. Each day army trucks drove us back and forth to our headquarters inside the old city gates. We were always under strict guard and not allowed to go sightseeing or wandering about the city. No dating. No shopping—there was nothing to buy anyway. There was only a small group of WACs in Nürnberg. I had not known any of them before, and I was there for such a short time that I made no close friends. For the most part, it was a dull life—working eight to five in the office, and not much else. Most of our time and thoughts were spent wondering how soon we would receive those magic orders saying we had enough points to go home.

The hate-filled eyes of the people of Nürnberg made chills go up and down our spines. Their sour glances made goose bumps grow on the backs of our necks. The people of Nürnberg never smiled. If they glanced in our direction, their look was a glare of open hatred: There were a lot of strong feelings because of the terrible bombings of Germany during the last stages of the war and because of the upcoming trials of war criminals. We were glad to be protected by the strict army rules. After months of sporadic raids, three straight nights of RAF bombing and two days of our Eighth and Ninth Army Air Force bombing had ended the war in Nürnberg. There were so many deaths that Americans in the nearby POW camps had been forced to dig graves for their German captors for weeks during these raids—which was no easy task as malnourished and poorly clothed as these prisoners were. We could understand how the Germans felt, but it was most uncomfortable to be there. Nürnberg must have been a beautiful city before the war. Now it was a dour, miserable, depressing place. (A friend of mine who was a prisoner of war near Nürnberg near the end of the war has told me, "You got this paragraph exactly as it was." He lost all his hair and nails from the diet of rutabaga soup he was fed in this camp.)

The Nürnberg war crime trials began in November 1945 and lasted until 1949. (I'm glad I wasn't there during those days.)

To help our morale, an army truck and driver were sent to our barracks one Sunday morning to take anyone who wanted to go on a picnic up into the foothills of the Alps in Bavaria. It was a warm, sunny late summer day, so fifteen of us clambered into the back of the truck with the huge lunch packed for us by the army cooks. They had even put in three crates of fresh oranges, the first fresh fruit we had seen in months, and we wolfed all that luscious fruit down before the day ended.

The truck sped along the autobahns of southern Germany. These highways were very impressive even in wartime: wide, well built, well marked, safe for fast speeds. In spite of the wonderful roads, we met only one or two cars that were not U.S. Army vehicles. The Germans had expended all their gasoline and oil in a last-ditch effort to win the war. We saw hundreds of camouflaged German planes, all in perfect shape, parked in patches of woods along the roads, unused because they lacked fuel.

We had driven many miles through the foothills without seeing another vehicle when suddenly we came upon three or four army trucks parked along the side of the road. As we came closer, we noticed a number of GIs standing at the edge of the road and in the nearby woods.

"Oh, look! A bunch of American GIs," someone said.

"What the heck are they doing, anyway? Everyone's got their backs to us."

"Oh, oh. Just a call-of-nature stop!"

"Come on, girls. Let's wave at them!"

Inspiration struck. We shouted with laughter as we called to the soldiers.

"Whatcha doin', GI?"

"Where ya from?"

"Why don't you wave at us and be friendly?"

"Keep up the good work, men!"

And together we sang, "I know what you're doin'."

Those poor GIs couldn't help laughing, too, but I never saw so many red faces in one spot. Our driver obliged us by slowing down and honking as we passed the trucks, and then speeding away. I'm sure those embarrassed men could hear us laughing for miles.

We sang as we drove along through gorgeous mountain foothills covered with trees, flowers, and with fantastic views of the Alps to the south. The peaceful picnic on a high wooded overlook near the mountains was heaven after the tensions in Nürnberg.

Reality hit us again on our way back to the base when we drove through what had once been a medium-sized city named Ulm. I do not know what the reason had been, but Ulm had obviously been the target of some of our heaviest bombings. In the main section of the town there was total devastation. For at least a whole square mile, nothing was left standing, just low piles of rubble. No trees, not even remnants of walls. Piles and piles of shattered bricks and broken timbers. Only one thing over three feet high was left standing in that huge area—a church. At a distance its towers and walls seemed whole as they guarded over the remnants of the city, but on coming closer we could see that the church had no roof or windows, and the walls were riddled with shell holes. It must have been a beautiful church before the bombing. Now, it epitomized the horror and sadness and senselessness of war.

DACHAU

I can never, ever, forget another trip I took while stationed in Germany. That summer, a group of us were given a chance to visit the concentration camp at Dachau, which the American troops had liberated only a short time before, on April 29, 1945. We had heard stories about this death camp, but nothing prepared us for the sheer horror of actually seeing the place.

The prisoners were all gone by that time, and a lot of the cleanup work had been done—but not all of it. I remember that day as cold and dark and gloomy, but maybe it just seemed that way in that awful place. As we drove in through the gates and past the high barbed wire fences, we saw a bare muddy area with a number of shabby barracks. Some of these buildings were just as they had been left by the prisoners, jammed with double-deck bunks, no bedding or mattresses, broken windows, and cracks in the walls letting in the cold wind. Other buildings, in better condition, looked like offices. A railroad siding ended near the middle of the area, and empty kennels lined a back fence. Immediately after taking over the camp, the Americans had killed all the vicious dogs that had been housed there. These dogs had been trained to hunt out and kill prisoners attempting to escape.

Then we saw that large concrete building with thick walls. That infamous gas chamber! I could visualize the hundreds of Jews, Gypsies, and other "unwanted" people—men, women, and children—who had been crowded into this box of a room, naked and frightened, the heavy steel door slammed shut and locked, and then killed by Zyklon-B, the poisonous gas pellets pumped in from overhead vents. The cement floor sloped to a drain in the center for easy cleaning. Blood stains covered the walls seven or eight feet high. And there were deep scratches in the thick concrete walls where frantic dying people had tried to claw their way to safety with their bare hands.

Outside this room and a few hundred feet to the north stood the oven in which thousands of human bodies had been cremated. It looked like the laundry stove in my grandmother's basement, only much larger, with a tall chimney reaching high into the sky. I was surprised that this furnace was not larger, but it had done its gruesome work quite efficiently, turning thousands and thousands of people into ashes.

Oh, the ashes! Piles of ashes everywhere around the oven. Little sifts of ashes blown around by the wind. People's ashes everywhere.

And the smell of the place! The smell of the ashes. And the horrible pungent smell of disinfectants. The fetid smells of death. Thousands upon thousands of deaths. When the ovens were going, the sickening stench must have spread miles and miles downwind. How could the local people possibly claim that they did not know about this piece of hell!

The American soldiers who had liberated this camp found some of the prisoners barely alive; they were mere skeletons, sick and clad in ragged striped concentration camp uniforms, barely able to move. The liberators also found huge piles of dead bodies heaped carelessly, waiting to be burned, although the Germans had tried desperately to get rid of all the bodies in last-minute around-the-clock burning. The huge mass grave the Americans had dug for the remainder of the bodies made a hill near the incinerator.

Thousands of Jews and other camp inmates had been used as guinea pigs at Dachau in many kinds of medical and "scientific" experiments, most of which were merely sadistic. Nazi doctors performed various bizarre techniques and surgeries. For instance, one doctor conducted countless amputations without anesthetic, then sent the cripples to the gas chamber. Another doctor experimented with the effects of low air pressure on humans by hanging prisoners up in an air chamber until their lungs burst. Victims were infected with various animal viruses to watch reactions—no matter if they died. The skin of some prisoners was made into lampshades, purses, and other objects much prized by the guards and camp commandants. Women and children were tortured in numerous other imaginative and even more gruesome ways. Such horrors went on and on and on. So many awful things happened in this camp that it would take hundreds of volumes to list them all.

In my imagination that day, I could see the vicious dogs, the even more vicious guards, the beatings and tortures. I could almost hear voices begging for mercy, screaming, moaning. For years after this visit my nights were haunted by nightmares of death and torture.

After this trip, I didn't feel so guilty when the German people glared at me.

COMING HOME

In early September 1945, after nearly two years in the ETO but only six weeks after arriving in Nürnberg, I finally received orders saying I had acquired the necessary service points to get a free ride home to the States. A few days later, I caught an air force plane to Orly field in Paris, then on to England, and home aboard the Queen Mary. I was to have a round trip in this great ship.

This voyage was very different from the trip over. There was no zigzagging now that the danger of submarines was over. The September weather in the North Atlantic is much better than the storms of winter, so the ride was much smoother. The voyage took much less time, five days instead of seven.

The Queen Mary was filled with servicemen returning home, with only twenty-five or thirty WACs aboard. There was not much fraternizing or flirting. We were all too tired and worn out and too anxious to get home. I spent most of the time just staring over the railing at the ocean, my mind in neutral. The foam on the crests of the waves reminded me of the ballet lines

I had seen in London, and the deep, heavy fogs were like England, too.

The last morning, word spread rapidly that the Statue of Liberty was in sight. Everyone raced to that side of the ship, and there, standing proud in the sunshine, her arm raised in greeting, was the Lady herself. I had not expected my reaction to the sight. I thought I was too numb, too weary, to get very excited over seeing just another statue.

But I cried. And so did most of the rest of the WACs and GIs on board.

POSTSCRIPT

AFTER THE WAR WAS OVER

World War II in Europe ended at 1:41 A.M. on May 7, 1945, when the Germans surrendered to the Allies. The official ceremonies took place in Reims, France.

The war was fought on five continents.

Millions of lives had been lost.

President Roosevelt was dead, and Harry Truman was now president of the United States. Mussolini had been killed. Hitler died three weeks after Roosevelt's death.

A long, difficult, bloody struggle was finally ended.

On September 15, 1945, Corporal Grace V. Porter, army serial number A-702462, was honorably discharged from the Headquarters Squadron of the Forty-second Air Depot Group at Fort Sheridan, Illinois.

I had served as a cryptographic technician in the campaigns of Normandy, Northern France, Rhineland, Central Europe, and Air Offensive Europe.

My decorations and citations included a European-African-Middle Eastern Theater ribbon with one silver battle star, the WAAC service ribbon, three overseas service bars, and a good conduct medal.

I served in the Women's Army Auxiliary Corps (WAAC) for five months and twenty-six days before enlisting in the reg-

147

ular army on September 1, 1943. Foreign service time was one year six months twenty-nine days. My length of service for pay purposes did not include the time served in the WAAC.

I received $300 mustering out pay and $19.20 travel pay from Fort Sheridan to my home in Iowa.

Approximately 140,000 American women served on active military duty in the WACs during World War II, and there were also thousands of women volunteers in the naval services.

These women who served their country well came home without honors or recognition. Women veterans have been shortchanged all along the way.

Many of these women had health problems because of their service, but army hospitals around the country had no facilities to take care of them. No effort was made to provide medical care for women veterans until the late 1980s, and even those efforts were pitifully few and ineffective, involving very few hospitals or care centers.

In my own case, my health was permanently damaged during my service. I will always have problems with my digestive system as a result of the stress and the poor food I endured during the war. I have severe migraine headaches and arthritis in my legs, which also can be traced to my army days. And I have had a great many sleep problems and nightmares about bombings, dead bodies, lost friends, and the other realities of wartime Europe. For years after the war, my memories would often wake me from a sound sleep, and I would cry uncontrollably.

WELCOME BACK, SECOND-CLASS SOLDIER

At the dock in New York, there were bands, proud speeches, and applause for "our fighting men." No mention whatsoever was made of the returning women, and we all felt brushed aside, ignored. However, we were tired—and it was so good to be home! So we concentrated on the pleasure of being back in the "good old USA" instead of complaining about our lack of welcome. We had marched in a great parade in Belgium, so another one wasn't really necessary.

Long tables were set up on the dock in New York by the Red Cross. We were served a huge breakfast with all the foods we had missed for so long: bacon, eggs, fresh orange juice, toasted white bread with real butter and jam, fresh fruits, and much more. And even huge bowls of ice cream afterward! The only problem was that this all tasted so good to us, after craving it for so long, that we overate. Some couldn't stop drinking milk, and some tried to eat several servings of ice cream. Our stomachs were not used to this food, so it was inevitable that many of us became very sick even after small helpings.

I was sent by train to Fort Sheridan, Illinois, the closest army post to my home in Iowa, for mustering out. Within a few short days, I was declared a civilian once more.

I returned home to Vinton, Iowa, with its tall elm trees, quiet streets, and Green Giant cannery (for corn, peas, and asparagus). My father, a World War I veteran and hero, was tremendously proud of me. Soon after I got back, he insisted that I join the American Legion Post where he had been an active member for years. My mother agreed. I was proud of my service and glad to be able to join the ranks of war veterans and do something that would please my father and make my family proud.

The local American Legion Post officers were taken aback at this invasion of their male territory and questioned at length my qualifications for membership. Finally, finding no valid excuse for refusing my application, and realizing that I wasn't going away, they reluctantly agreed to accept me as a member. My father proudly escorted me to my first meeting. I was properly dressed in my uniform, complete with all the ribbons and stars I had earned.

An abbreviated initiation ceremony, mumbled quickly, made me an official member of the American Legion. The rest of the evening was a disaster. No one but my father spoke to me. The other men refused even to look in my direction. I was pointedly ignored, even when my father tried to introduce me around to his "friends."

My father was so crushed, so embarrassed, so sorry for me that we left early. He never again mentioned the Legion to me. I received no further communication from the post: no meeting notices, nothing. It was as though that evening had never happened.

Decades later, I asked about joining the Veterans of Foreign Wars post in Harlem, Montana. I was told that I would have to join the VFW auxiliary as a wife, a mother, or a daughter of a veteran.

But I *was* a bonafide veteran! I was not just a family member, although I qualified in all three categories for the auxiliary (I have mentioned my father's service; my husband was a combat veteran of World War II, serving four years in the navy on the USS *Chicago* in the South Pacific; and my son was an officer with the 101st Division in Vietnam for over a year).

Then, in 1965, I was invited to a ceremony in Great Falls, Montana, honoring women veterans. The evening was planned by Norma Ashby, a TV show hostess. The program was presented by personnel from the Great Falls Air Base, with speeches by base officers. An excellent dinner was served. There was entertainment. It was all very nice. After recognizing women in all the other various branches of the armed services, a male air force officer asked for veterans of the Women's Army Auxiliary Air Force to stand—he didn't even get the name right: It was the Women's Army Air Force, and definitely not an auxiliary. I was the only member there, so I stood up . . . and kept my mouth shut as the officer rushed on to the next category.

That evening was the first time I was ever recognized publicly as an authentic veteran.

Throughout these fifty years since World War II, I have had to endure hundreds of conversations like this:

Ex-GI: *Things were really rough when I was in the army* [or navy or marines]. *Two years of hell!*

Me: *Where did you serve?*

Ex-GI: *Well, most of the time was in El Centro, California* [or Wichita, Kansas, or Juneau, Alaska], *and believe me, that's a real hellhole! No decent place for my wife to live. Prices sky high. Standing room only in all the bars. Hot as Hades* [or cold as the North Pole]. *Couldn't wait to get home again.*

Me: *I was in the army, too. In Europe.* (I would say this in a friendly way, clearly and loudly enough that I knew he could hear. But he would always continue as though I had not spoken.)

Ex-GI: *Yep. We had to spend a full half a day every damn week just drilling. We got so bored we played a lot of poker. Couldn't save much money. But me and my buddies sure had fun.*

And he would drift off into some story about a good leave or a good drunk or a mean officer.

Me: *Sounds rough.* (Sigh.)

Ex-GI: *Oh, it was!* (In a suffering tone.)

Even conversations with servicemen who had been overseas followed the same pattern. Refusal to acknowledge that women might have made contributions to the war effort. Never any interest in what I might have done or seen.

Oh, well. Who knows: Maybe El Centro really *was* hell.

I have often tried to understand these responses. Perhaps men find it impossible to include women in their memories of the service: Girls aren't supposed to fight; women aren't supposed to be soldiers. Perhaps men think that acknowledgment that women served in the armed forces overseas during wartime would somehow detract from their own achievements as males. Or maybe they still believe some of the scurrilous rumors about the morals of women in the service.

I have seldom argued with the "suffering" GIs. It always seemed so futile: If I said anything, it only stirred up animosity, so it has always been easier to let it pass. It was water under the bridge, and nothing was to be achieved by fighting the world about it. I was too busy rebuilding my own life to bother about such things.

Then, after my subconscious had nagged me for years, suddenly a few words on a well-known national news program jolted me into writing this story at last.

One Sunday evening in January 1989, this program presented a short story about a memorial being proposed in Washington, D.C., to honor army nurses. *How nice,* I thought. *They deserve something like that.* A small plaque with names of nurses killed in wartime was being discussed, to be set somewhere near the Vietnam Memorial.

However, a faction in Washington opposed this memorial, the commentator reported. A Washington lawmaker was quoted, *Ah, let's give 'em a little plaque somewhere and end the argument. And then maybe put a plaque right next to it for the Canine Corps.*

My blood pressure shot sky high. My face got red, my hands shook. Seldom have I been so angry! How *could* they equate American servicewomen with dogs! Why was the loss of the life or the service-time of an American woman of so little consequence in comparison to the loss of the life or the service-time of an American man? Why was the time a man spent in the armed forces of his country worth so much more than a woman's service in the same time and place? At that moment, if I could have reached the fool in Washington who made that statement, his life would have been in jeopardy.

Nurses who serve in war zones deserve full credit for their courage, suffering, and depredations. They are all volunteers. They are indispensable members of our armed forces and have earned all the respect and honor that is accorded to any soldier, sailor, or marine.

But, not to minimize the contributions nurses have made, at least *they* have received some credit and recognition for their service. Various books, movies, and TV shows have pointed out the hardships and problems nurses endured at Bataan, Corregidor, and other battles and prison camps, making the public more aware of their great dedication and service to our country.

Now . . . how many TV shows, books, movies, or news stories have you ever seen that showed the real contributions of the other women—not the nurses—in the army? The only one I know of is *Private Benjamin*, which made a mockery of the women's services. It is comedy—no more, no less—a vehicle to show Goldie Hawn in a standardized comic role with a slightly different setting.

Vietnam veterans rightly feel they have never received the recognition they deserve from their country for serving well and honorably in a very nasty little war in which very few of them believed.

I contend that women veterans of the various services have received even less recognition and gratitude from their country and countrymen for service that also was hard and uncomfortable and demanding. Scant attention has been paid to their sacrifices and contributions to the United States.

So I was jolted. Well, I decided, it's time I started on the book my kids have been coaxing me to write about my life in the army. Maybe women veterans haven't made enough effort to tell their side of things. Only recently has an effort has been made to build a women-in-service memorial at the gates of Arlington Cemetery.

So here is my contribution to their story and to the many, many heroes of World War II: our men and women in the various armed services; their families who worked hard on the home front to support them; the armed forces of our allies; and the suffering, valiant people of England and Europe.

There were so many heroes.

And so much pain.